Spiritual gates to he. sons and daughters. Kevin Basconi was taken to heaven to teach you how to access these gates!

SID ROTH
Host, "It's Supernatural!"

Some of you are not content with where you are in your Christian walk. Some of you have been believing for the **MORE** but you have *not seen* the fulfillment of your hope. If you are among those, then this book is for you! The age to come is seeping into our reality and you can jump in with both feet and experience the goodness of God. *Unlocking the Hidden Mysteries of the Powers of the Age to Come* is an anointed guidebook for what you have been longing to see in your life.

PAUL L. COX
Aslan's Place, Apple Valley, California

We can all glean from Kevin's extraordinary prophetic experiences and outstanding revelation. I've discovered that the more you access these mysteries, the more impartation you will receive for victory! *Unlocking the Hidden Mysteries of the Powers of the Age to Come* is a provocation into a higher dimension of sight, sound and perception—a supernatural invitation to come up higher to walk in the glory and goodness of God!

JOSHUA MILLS
Best-selling Author, **Time & Eternity**

This is a deeply personal account of the author's journey into the glory of God and detailed depictions of his experiences of the open heavens. This new work by Kevin Basconi is filled with testimonies, prayers, and impartation to help others discover all these things for themselves.

Kevin encourages others to stop waiting and begin their own journey of exploration into the deep mysteries of the Kingdom of God. In *Unlocking the Hidden Mysteries of the Powers of the Age to Come*, a powerful witness is released to help you understand that you can also have similar spiritual experiences.

The author clearly points the way for you to *see* what he has seen and releases you to experience even more. If you are seeking deeper experience in the glory realms, this book is for you! If you want to live under the blessings of God that flow from an open heaven, this book is for you!

PASTOR JAMES DURHAM
Higher Calling Ministries International

Kevin Basconi has once again written a powerful book on the mysteries of God's supernatural Kingdom. This book will challenge you and spur you into higher dimensions of God's glory as well as challenge you to go beyond your current experience and knowledge of God. This could be the very book that propels you into the greater dimensions of God that you have been waiting for until now!

DR. DAVID HERZOG
*President of D.H.M., Author of **Glory Invasion***

I am honored and blessed to be a friend and fellow worker with Kevin and Kathy Basconi as we work together to share the love of Jesus Christ with those who will receive Him. Kevin and Kathy are people of integrity who live the principles they teach. In his new book, *Unlocking the Hidden Mysteries of the Powers of the Age to Come*, Kevin shares extraordinary experiences and delves deeply and gives insight into the meaning and application to world events and for the Body of Christ today.

DR. STEPHEN R. RICHARDSON
Ordained Foursquare minister and medical doctor, retired

Unlocking the Hidden Mysteries of the Powers of the Age to Come is all about taking hidden truths and making them plain. The Bible says that *"it is the glory of God to conceal a matter, But the glory of kings is to search out a matter"* (Proverbs 25:2, NKJV). Kevin Basconi is one who has searched out mysteries, discovered practical keys, and is now communicating those truths in ways for others to walk in. There are two primary things I love about Kevin's books. First, there are many practical examples of what he is has come to understand. It is not just theoretical or theological concepts he explains but practical truths that have an effect on our daily lives. Second, it is always evident that Kevin wants the reader to walk in or experience what he is conveying. He challenges us with "the whosoever anointing" and "the Kingdom of God within you." It is not just Kevin who experiences these encounters; it is for all of us!

I recommend *Unlocking the Hidden Mysteries of the Powers of the Age to Come* to you. It will put a hunger in you not only for "God experiences" but will also arouse a passion for the Father, Jesus, and Holy Spirit. A fire will be stirred in you!

PASTOR ALAN KOCH
Senior Pastor, Christ Triumphant Church

It is with great enthusiasm we partake of Kevin's new book, *Unlocking the Hidden Mysteries of the Powers of the Age to Come*, and what the Lord has given him. We say; Yes! We look forward to an outpouring of the fullness of the Spirit with love, peace, and mercy and God's glory revealed in a time when the shaking of the world is happening. You will be blessed!

PASTOR PER AND MAJBRITT ALTSVED
Stockholm, Sweden

Kevin Basconi and his loving wife, Kathy, are first of all dear people of the Lord. Secondly, they are dear friends to me and to Victorious Living Fellowship. Kevin has been chosen to come near to God as the scriptures teach us in Psalm 65:4: *"Blessed is the man whom thou choosest, and causest to approach unto thee, that he may dwell in thy courts: we shall be satisfied with the goodness of thy house, even of thy holy temple"* (KJV).

This verse declares such a blessed man *"shall be satisfied with the goodness of thy house"* (KJV). Kevin has been favored by the Lord to eat from the Lord's heavenly table. He has captured these experiences in his Seer Trilogy that I strongly recommend that everyone reads. What Kevin was shown while in the heavenly places, the Lord instructed him to share upon the earth. I have had the privilege of tasting heavenly substance in this book, *Unlocking the Hidden Mysteries of the Powers of the Age to Come*. Kevin has been fruitful and generous to share generously the "goodness" of the tables and of the courts of heaven with others.

The revelation that he reveals in this book is very rich and full of life! It imparted into me a stronger desire to approach the heavenly places for myself. It will also inspire you as well. Kevin is a forerunner sent to infuse the Body of Christ with faith to experience the secret places of the heavenly realms I encourage you to eat from the table of the Lord that has been spread before you through Kevin's new book. You heart will be well nourished and inspired. May it be said of all of us who desire to be with the Lord, "*Thou has ascended on high...thou has received gifts for men.*"

DR. VICTORY MORGAN
Pastor, Victorious Living Fellowship, Orlando, Florida

This book will stir a desire up in your heart to know the power and presence of God in a greater way, as Kevin unfolds to you his personal encounters with the living God. I was in attendance at his School of the Seers 2013, when the entire gathering of 300 people was taken into the heavenly dimensions; and I testify that I have never experienced anything so real and powerful. It will give you understanding and revelation on how to establish spiritual truths in your own life.

CAROL KOCH
Director and Founder of Children on the Frontlines

Unlocking the
Hidden Mysteries
of the
Powers
of the
Age to Come
The Shaking &
The Arising!

Unlocking the
Hidden Mysteries

of the

Powers

of the

Age to Come

The Shaking &
The Arising!

KEVIN BASCONI

ISBN: 978-0-9960217-2-2

King of Glory Ministries International Publications 2015
King of Glory Ministries International
PO Box 903, Moravian Falls, NC 28654
336-818-1210
www.kingofgloryministries.org

Unless otherwise noted, all scripture quotations are from the New King James Version of the Bible. Copyright © 1979, 1980, 1982 by Thomas Nelson, Inc., publishers. Used by permission.

Scripture quotations marked NIV are from the Holy Bible, New International Version. Copyright © 1973, 1978, 1984, 2010, 2011, International Bible Society. Used by permission.

Scripture quotations marked ASV are from the American Standard Bible. Copyright © 1960, 1962, 1968, 1971, 1972, 1973, 1975, by the Lockman Foundation. Used by permission.

Scripture quotations marked ESV are from the Holy Bible, English Standard Version, copyright © 2001 by Crossway Bibles, a division of Good News Publisher. Used by permission.

Scripture quotations marked GW are from *God's Word*® Translation, ©1995 by God's Word to the Nations. All rights reserved.

Greek definitions are derived from Strong's Greek Concordance.
Hebrew definitions are derived from Strong's Hebrew Concordance.

Cover design and layout by Kevin Basconi & projectluz.com
Printed in the United States of America

This

book

Is

dedicated

to

God the Father, God the Son, and God the Holy Spirit

without

You

Guys

none

of

this

would

have

been

possible!

Table of Contents

Acknowledgements

I want to thank my wonderful precious wife, Kathy Basconi. Thank you for your enduring and everlasting love, your Christ-like kindness, your amazing patience, and for the long hours of proofreading. Thank you for your help and support with the entire process of writing these books.

You are more precious than rubies, and nothing that I may desire can compare with you or your love.

I love you!

I also want to thank my friend Paul Cox. Paul is a true seer and a true saint. Thank you, Paul, for your sincere help and allowing the love of God to be shed abroad in your heart by the Spirit of the Living God. Thank you, Paul; may the Lord richly bless you.

A special thank you to my friend Michael Danforth, who can look beyond what is seen and discern the reality of the true circumstances beyond our control and has encouraged me to entertain the heavenly realms to see what must take place after this (life). Thank you, Michael; may the Lord richly bless you.

Introduction
By Michael Danforth

The Body of Christ is continually advancing toward spiritual maturation. This is partially due to many spiritual leaders who are not afraid to share their personal experiences in conjunction with the word of God.

Kevin Basconi is one of such people. In his own right, he is a forerunner in the Kingdom of God. For a number of years, I have been privileged to participate with Kevin in various conferences, as well as, read the many great books he as has written during the course of his ministry. Once again, Kevin challenges the body of Christ to advance to the next level of spiritual maturity.

In this book, *Unlocking the Hidden Mysteries of the Powers of the Age to Come*, Kevin draws special attention to spiritual gates. This is certainly in sync with the times we are now in. In this year and the years to come, the subject of gates will become the epicenter of spiritual engagement.

In Old Testaments times the object of gates to a city or fortress was to fortify the intentions of a king or governing functions toward the people. Ezekiel describes how the king of Tyre was determined to take captive the nation of Israel.

Ezekiel quotes Tyre as mockingly saying, "*Aha, the gateway of the peoples is broken, it has opened to me. I shall be filled, now that she is laid waste*" (Ezekiel 26:2, ASV).

Here we can see the enemy's desire to break through the gateways of God, which indeed are the people, for the sole purpose of harnessing the treasure in them for his own evil intent.

David writes, "*Lift up your heads, O gates, and be lifted up, O ancient doors, that the King of glory may come in!*" (Psalm 24:7, ESV).

Another definition for the Hebrew word gate, *shahar*, is realm. Therefore, it could be said that we are the realms of heaven on earth. Wherever we go, the realms of God's kingdom go with us.

Thus the words of Jesus in speaking to Peter, "*On this rock I will build my church. And the gates of hell will not overpower it*" (Matthew 16:18, GW). In other words, unlike ancient times, the realms of hell will not overpower the realms of heaven that reside in the people of God.

You are the prevailing force of heaven on earth. The power of restoration that was released through the life of Jesus Christ is currently restoring the countless gates that have been broken down.

I am confident that Kevin's insight concerning the gates of God and multiple other kingdom mysteries revealed in this book will undoubtedly lead you into a greater depth of understanding the intent of God for your life and all that He has destined for you in this hour.

Michael Danforth is founder of Mountain Top International Ministries International and the School of Higher Learning in Yakima, Washington. He is a prophet, seer, psalmist, author, and revelatory speaker, focusing on increasing our awareness of all God has given us through the death and life of Jesus Christ and accessing that inheritance now.

CHAPTER 1

A Holy Hush

The heavens opened early on the Day of Atonement and the Lord began to speak. A holy hush filled the room as the evening sun began to dance upon the leaves of the oak trees outside of my window. The glory of God began to manifest and roll into my prayer room as if it were waves. A gentle breeze ruffled the leaves outside, and they seemed to dance and worship God as a Spirit of holiness and awe permeated my space. The leaves seemed to sing and dance; "Holy, holy, holy" reverberated through the spirit as they sang in unity and harmony. A supernatural peace filled my spirit and my soul seemed to magnify the Lord with His creation outside the window of my little prayer closet. Psalm 34:3 bubbled up from within me: "*Oh, magnify the LORD with me, And let us exalt His name together.*" For a moment all of creation seemed to exalt and worship the Lamb of God.

The heavens seemed to stir and a gentle wind began to blow in a circular pattern releasing the fragrances of heaven into my space. I lay upon my sheepskin prayer rug pondering the events of the last few weeks. (I had longed for a prayer rug like this one since I visited the resting place of the late evangelist Robert Sheffey on the one-hundredth anniversary of his death in 2002.) Surely this was a divine set up and God was going to come again. Another Yom Kippur and another visitation of the Lord's presence and goodness were at hand. Tears filled my eyes as God's goodness and faithfulness filled my heart. *"I will praise the name of God with a song, And today I magnify Him with thanksgiving"* (Psalm 69:30). It seemed at that moment that the whole earth was praising the Lord!

Psalm 113

Praise the LORD! Praise, O servants of the LORD, Praise the name of the LORD! Blessed be the name of the LORD From this time forth and forevermore! From the rising of the sun to its going down The LORD's name is to be praised. The LORD is high above all nations, His glory above the heavens. Who is like the LORD our God, Who dwells on high, Who humbles Himself to behold The things that are in the heavens and in the earth? He raises the poor out of the dust, And lifts the needy out of the ash heap, That He may seat him with princes—With the princes of His people. He grants the barren woman a home, Like a joyful mother of children. Praise the LORD!

As we learn to praise the Lord in the midst of trial and victories, we will begin to experience the breakthroughs and the supernatural manifestations of the Kingdom of Heaven! *"And the first voice which I heard was like a trumpet speaking with me, saying, 'Come up here, and I will show you things which must take place after this'"* (Revelation 4:1).

I began to tremble as the glory filled the room. It seemed as if shofars were sounding in the heavenly realms and the veil between heaven and earth shook and trembled. In fact, I saw the veil tremble with anticipation as if it were a pregnant woman whose water has broken and whose time had come. In the spirit I saw this supernatural barrier between heaven and earth shimmering with translucence and becoming incredibly porous at that instant. The veil is about to rip open forever!

Once again the ground seemed to shake and vibrate here in Moravian Falls. The ground has been shaking for weeks now in many cities and in many nations, and the whole earth groans for the birthing of the true sons and daughters of God.

In fact, it seemed as if the whole earth was groaning and awaiting the manifestation of the Kingdom of God. As the glory lingered, the Holy Spirit whispered into my ear, *"For the earnest expectation of the creation eagerly waits for the revealing of the sons of God"* (Romans 8:19).

In the spirit I sensed many doors opening. The key of David is being released to God's children at this hour to open doors and to shut doors (Isaiah 22:22). The Lord is opening doors that no man can shut and closing other doors that no man can open. What a glorious time to be alive!

The Kingdom of Heaven is truly at hand. The time has come for the manifestation of the true sons and daughters of the Most High God. "They are coming," says the Lord. The Holy Spirit began to speak to me very clearly as the last vestiges of the sun began to wane. Glorious Golden rays of the evening sunshine painted the worshiping oak leaves' brilliant hues, and the branches of the trees seemed to glow and clap their hands in rhythm with the Spirit of Almighty God.

> *"My chosen ones are arising even now. They will not look like what many expect. No, I will raise up the most unlikely," says the Lord. "The discarded, the forgotten, the broken, the contrite, the hopeless, the least likely; these will be my jewels. These I will endue with heavenly power and revelation. I will use them in unusual power and demonstrations of My Spirit and of My Kingdom. They are coming, even now. The rulers of this age are passing away, and a new generation is arising to take their place. They will walk in holiness and with My authority. They will rise up into the heavenlies and see and hear what must take place after this. They shall bring the wisdom of men to nothing, and the foolishness of this age will be destroyed. The Kingdom of God shall arise and the kingdom of man shall tumble and fall. The shaking is coming! The shaking is coming! No one can hide from the wrath that is to come. Only in Me is there safety and salvation," says the Lord. "Seek Me while I may still be found. Seek Me before the end is come."*

Heaven is beginning to invade the earth (repeatedly). The frequency of this dynamic is only increasing. There is an acceleration in the heavenly realms, and the Lord is moving forward with His plans to return. Get ready!

CHAPTER 2

A Call from Sweden

This afternoon I spoke to my friend Pastor Per Altsved in Stockholm. It was 7:38 p.m., September 13, 2013, in Sweden. As we spoke I saw the parabola of the earth. Per said, "Yom Kippur has just started here." His words launched me into a supernatural vision. I was taken up into the seer realm, and in this vision I saw the earth far below. I saw Scandinavia. The glory of God was pouring out there. God's glory continued to roll across the earth as the evening sun began to set on Yom Kippur 2013.

God was pouring out His mercy and His grace upon the earth. God is pouring out His glory for all to see. Yet I also understood that the Lord was pouring out His judgments. The days of awe are ending and the days of God's judgments are beginning to come into full fruition. Yet, God's judgments are full of His mercy. God's judgments are perfect as the Lord is perfect. God's judgments are pure just as His word is pure. The Lord is calling for His people to be pure and walk in holiness. God is calling His people to judge with righteous judgments (John 7:24).

The Lord is calling His creation to repentance. The Lord is calling His creation (mankind—the creature) into a place of communion and intimacy. We can no longer live far from the God of the universe, Elohim. God Almighty has been giving the whole earth a grace to return to Him. Yet, many nations have hardened their hearts and turned a deaf ear to the Spirit of God.

This will be a season that judgments will begin to accelerate upon the earth—in individuals, in ministries, in states, and in nations. The Lord of Host's angelic reapers are being released to walk across the earth to discern the state of the hearts of men and the state of the nations. The plumb line is in their hands. Even now nations will begin to crumble and others will falter and fall. Mighty harvester angels are being loosed from the throne room of our great King. Zechariah 4 is a timely prophetic portrait for our day.

Zechariah 4:1-14

Now the angel who talked with me came back and wakened me, as a man who is wakened out of his sleep. And he said to me, "What do you see?" So I said, "I am looking, and there is a lampstand of solid gold with a bowl on top of it, and on the stand seven lamps with seven pipes to the seven lamps. Two olive trees are by it, one at the right of the bowl and the other at its left." So I answered and spoke to the angel who talked with me, saying, "What are these, my lord?" Then the angel who talked with me answered and said to me, "Do you not know what these are?" And I said, "No, my lord." So he answered and said to me: "This is the word of the LORD to Zerubbabel: 'Not by might nor by power, but by My Spirit,' Says the LORD of hosts. 'Who are you, O great mountain? Before Zerubbabel you shall become a plain! And he shall bring forth the capstone With shouts of "Grace, grace to it!"'" Moreover the word of the LORD came to me, saying: "The hands of Zerubbabel Have laid the foundation of this temple; His hands shall also finish it. Then you will know That the LORD of hosts has sent Me to you. For who has despised the day of small things? For these seven rejoice to see The plumb line in the hand of Zerubbabel. They are the eyes of the LORD, Which scan to and fro throughout the whole earth." Then I answered and said to him, "What are these two olive trees-at the right of the lampstand and at its left?" And I further answered and said to him, "What are these two olive branches that drip into the receptacles of the two gold pipes from which the golden oil drains?" Then he answered me and said, "Do you not know what these are?" And I said, "No, my lord." So he said, "These are the two anointed ones, who stand beside the Lord of the whole earth."

God's Plumb Line

Though it is an hour of judgments, it is also a time of great grace for God's people. The Spirit of God is seeking those in whom He can dwell. The Lord Jesus is sending out the angels of the Lord to search throughout the whole earth seeking those who have clean hands and a pure heart. The Lord is looking for those who have not lifted up their soul to an idol nor sworn deceitfully. These are the ones to whom the Lord will release great grace and a greater power than we have ever experienced in the Body of Christ. This is the hour when God's people will learn to unlock the hidden mysteries of the Kingdom of Heaven when they set their hearts to seek Him, to be diligent to seek His face (see Psalm 24).

It will not be by their might, not their power, but by the Spirit of the Lord that they will conquer the issues and obstacles of this present age. God wants us to learn to be diligent and to rest in Him so that we can be established by His Spirit. He wants for us to allow the Spirit of God, the *ruwach* of God, to work on our behalf. At this place the enemy will just flee from us because he doesn't understand what we are doing as we are waiting upon the Lord; except he knows that we are talking to Papa and he needs to get out of there quick. The breath of God—*ruah ha-qodesh*—could come at any second, so he flees.

This supernatural exchange is illustrated in Zechariah 4:6: "'*Not by might nor by power, but by My Spirit,' Says the LORD of hosts.*" In this passage of scripture, the Hebrew words translated "might" and "power" can be defined as the force or means of man, human flesh and resources, human military strength, wealth, virtue, valor or courage, physical strength and/or man's physical ability. We could also say it means man's intellectual knowledge or the schemes and philosophies of the human mind.

So the Lord is declaring or prophesying to the seer prophet Zechariah through an angelic being:

This miraculous transformation is not going to happen because of your physical abilities or your military resilience. This miraculous exchange is not going to happen because of your intellectual way of life, worldly mindsets, or philosophies (doctrines). This miraculous exchange happens when you rest in Me and allow the Holy Spirit to move upon your behalf.

That can be difficult unless you learn to be diligent to enter into the rest of the Lord.

Perhaps you are in bondage to some sort of sin or generational iniquity as you read this. Resting in the Lord can set you free from generational sins and iniquities in a simple, effortless, supernatural exchange. You can be set free from religion or a religious spirit. So we could say that the amazing and miraculous transformation of your life and personal circumstances will not come from your ability to earn money or work with the strength and abilities of your hands. Your miraculous transformation is not going to manifest because of your superior intellectual ability and carnal mindsets of intellectual knowledge or the philosophies of psychologists, scientists, politicians, or theologians. Neither will the Body of Christ be transformed into a Christlike character by any of these human attributes.

Accessing the Rest of the Lord

The Lord of Hosts is saying that these kinds of miraculous transformations will come to pass supernaturally by the Spirit of God. These miraculous transformations are initiated by the *ruwach* of God. *Ruwach* is the Hebrew word translated "Spirit" in Zechariah 4:6. *Ruwach* is the breath, exhalation, or the breathed word of God. Remember that God breathed into the dust and created the creature man (see Genesis 2:7). In fact, it was the *ruwach* of God, or the Spirit of God, that was lingering or resting over the waters that supernaturally birthed all of creation in Genesis 1:2: "*The earth was without form, and void; and darkness was on the face of the deep. And the Spirit [ruwach] of God was hovering over the face of the waters.*"

We are talking about the word decrees and prayers of God. This is the very breath of God, or we could say God's breath of life. To say it another way, when Jesus Christ prays for you as *the* royal Priest according to the order of Melchizedek, He releases the *ruwach* of Father God or the God-ordained destiny or God-inspired prophetic word into and over your life. Jesus declares your destiny in the heavenly realms or dimensions. These decrees or *ruwach* of God then supernaturally manifest in the temporal or earthly dimension.

Of course, we need to walk in chronological and geographical obedience to God to position ourselves to receive these blessings. However, when God begins to speak from His throne of mercy, power, and grace, it is not by our might or our power but by the power of the Holy Spirit of the living God that this supernatural exchange takes place. When we learn to rest in the glory our lives are transformed, and new destinies are birthed and activated in the hovering of His glory of the Holy Ghost. The key to this process is resting in the fullness of the Lord and allowing the Spirit of God to move upon your behalf.

When we learn to be diligent to enter into meditative prayer and wait in the glory of God, then God begins to move upon our behalf as we learn to allow and release Jesus to intercede for us from the right hand of the Father, which is *the* place of **the** Power (Hebrews 8:34). When the Lord Jesus prays for us, then it is simply a matter of allowing the Lord's prayers to manifest as the Father releases the wonderful Holy Spirit to go forth and move upon our behalf. Sometimes we just need to wait and rest in the Lord while the Holy Spirit and the breath of the Holy Spirit is working on our behalf and in our sphere of influence and within our lives (Hebrews 4:10). The Holy Spirit will honor our God-ordained destiny when we enter into the rest of the Lord. The Father rested and allowed the *ruwach* of the Holy Spirit to work in the beginning of creation as recorded in Genesis 1:2. We can also honor the Holy Spirit by resting and allowing the Spirit of God to work on our behalf.

Excel in Strength

At other times the Lord will also release His angelic hosts to go forth and to make our paths straight and to co-labor or minister *for* us, who are to inherit Christ's salvation. We see this in Psalm 103:20: "*Bless the LORD, you His angels, Who excel in strength, who do His word, Heeding the voice of His word.*" At times God releases angels to help bring the intercession of Christ to come to pass in our lives (see Hebrews 1:14). The reason for this is that God's angels recognize the *ruwach* or breath of God on His words and work steadfastly to help those prophetic decrees manifest in your life. It is really very simple. We rest in the fullness of the Lord and allow God to work on our behalf. When we enter into the fullness of His rest, we learn to totally trust God by allowing the Spirit of God to work on our behalf in any form or fashion that the Lord chooses. At times this takes the form of pruning, and this can be uncomfortable (John 15:2).

This aspect of the rest of the Lord is spelled out for us in scripture. Hebrews 4 illustrates how Jesus Christ will intercede for us as a royal Priest according to the order of Melchizedek from His throne of rest and power to work on our behalf. That is what the seven angelic beings are doing at this hour. They have the plumb line of the Lord in their hands. They are seeking people like you who are hungry to know the hidden and mysterious things that God has concealed and kept back for you at this hour. They are searching for willing and sanctified vessels that the powers of the age to come can flow through.

The glory of God is rolling across and around the earth. The eyes of the Lord (the seven angels with the plumb line of the Lord) are seeking those who have clean hands and pure hearts. Great moves of God will spring up upon the earth, and many will see the power of God as He releases signs and wonders in the heavens above and upon the earth beneath. The judgments of God release His mercy, yet God will not always strive with man. Though there is still a season of grace, now is the time to return to the Lord; tomorrow may be too late.

I saw the glory of God roll across the face of the earth like a mighty tidal wave of God's grace and authority. I saw the Kingdom of God coming upon the earth as I spoke to my friend Per. I felt the power of God pour out in a mighty ways. I sensed that the spirit of holiness is now being released to Scandinavian and the European regions and to the Americas as well. It is not a time to reject the Spirit of God. It is a time to turn to Him and to intercede for our nations and our leaders. We can still change the course of events concerning our nations on our knees.

The windows and gates of heaven are opening and the great cloud of witnesses is beginning to descend into the earthly realms. God's heavenly family is becoming more and more active in the temporal or earthly realm. The heavens are opening and our heavenly family is being released to help prepare the way for the Lord's return (see Ephesians 3: 14-19).

There is an excitement in the spiritual realms. The heavenly hosts of God's family know that the return of the Messiah is close at hand and they are rejoicing! The great cloud of witnesses is eager to be released to invade the earthly dimensions to help the King of kings and the Lord of lords take His back His creation. At the same time the hordes of darkness also know that the time is near when the trump will sound and the end will come. First Thessalonians 4:16-18 illustrates this imminent outpouring of Christ's Kingdom upon the earth:

> For the Lord Himself will descend from heaven with a shout, with the voice of an archangel, and with the trumpet of God. And the dead in Christ will rise first. Then we who are alive and remain shall be caught up together with them in the clouds to meet the Lord in the air. And thus we shall always be with the Lord. Therefore comfort one another with these words.

The time is close at hand!

A Season of Judgments

The Lord is preparing His bride for His triumphant return! God can redeem His creation with an outstretched arm and with great judgments. True and righteous are the judgments of God. We are now entering into a God-ordained season of righteous judgments. *"Oh, the depth of the riches both of the wisdom and knowledge of God! How unsearchable are His judgments and His ways past finding out"* (Romans 11:33).

The shaking will continue! God will continue to shake the earth and the structures of the governments of the lands. Many nations, including America, will not be immune to divine shaking. Yet, in all of this is the love of God. The Lord has spoken to me very clearly about this dynamic on the Day of Atonement over the last few years. This is what He said. I believe that it bears repeating as the Day of the Lord draws near. The scriptures from Joel also refer to the coming of the great and terrible Day of the Lord.

Joel 2:1, 11, 31

Blow the trumpet in Zion, And sound an alarm in My holy mountain! Let all the inhabitants of the land tremble; For the day of the LORD is coming, For it is at hand.... The LORD gives voice before His army, For His camp is very great; For strong is the One who executes His word. For the day of the LORD is great and very terrible; Who can endure it? ...The sun shall be turned into darkness, And the moon into blood, Before the coming of the great and awesome day of the LORD.

It is a season of the blood moons. It is a season of retribution and a time to reap what has been sown in our nations. It is a season to draw close to God whilst He may still be found (Isaiah 55:6). However, in the midst of all of this shaking there remains hope. For those who know the Lord and draw close to Him, these can be some of the most amazing and prosperous times ever! Even the judgments of God are poured out in His love and mercy. Though the world around you may be shaken, it need not come near you. Only with your eyes will you see these things.

CHAPTER 3

Shake, Rattle, and Roll

As I waited upon the Lord, I knew that there was a great acceleration of the shaking that is coming upon the earth. Back in 2009 I had purposed in my heart to wait upon the Lord on the Day of Atonement asking Him to speak to me. I was amazed to find that He did want to speak to me and in fact the Holy Spirit literally paid a visit to our house!

At the end of the Day of Atonement, a large and violent whirlwind dropped from the heavenly realms to rend nearly every leaf off of one tulip poplar tree in our yard in West Meadows. I had just left my prayer room and was telling God that I did not feel qualified to share some of the revelation that had shown to me. In my heart I had asked the Lord for a sign; and as this thought slipped off my mind, a supernatural whirlwind appeared with great force. It descended strait down from the heavenly realms, and with it came a forceful and rumbling sound similar to a freight train! Every hair on my body stood on end!

This powerful heavenly whirlwind moved slowly from the east to the west across our yard in West Meadows. The deep rumbling sound seemed to shake the ground and our little cabin. Then it lifted back in the heavens roaring and with all the leaves of the tree swirling in its powerful vortex. I watched as it supernaturally disappeared almost instantly. I gazed at the spot where it vanished for a moment and watched a few leaves slowly flutter to the ground below. Immediately I repented and told the Lord that I would share the visions and soon began to scribe the events of Yom Kippur! Here is what the Lord spoke to me through His word and through visions September 27 and 28 in 2009.

The Lord revealed to me in no uncertain terms that an approaching shaking would come upon the whole earth. In hindsight I can see that we are now well into this divine paradigm and unfolding of God's plans.

In a vision I saw the planet earth "quake." I was high above the earth in the heavenly realms, and I saw a violent shaking of the planet. It shook as if a child was shaking a rattle! The earth rattled and rolled for an extended time. As I witnessed this vision, I realized that the Lord would begin to violently shake the earth and that the things that we thought we understood would be uprooted and our gallant and haughty attitude would be changed in a moment and in the twinkle of an eye.

The Lord will continue to shake the foundations of the entire earth. This will be a literal thing. God will shake the earth and there will be unusually powerful earthquakes in diverse and sundry places during the year 2009 and beyond. One reason for this is because the Lord of Glory will speak from His throne of mercy, judgment, and grace causing the earth to quake at the sound of God's judgments and voice.

When God speaks there are earthquakes and whirlwinds released upon the earth!

The Present Tense

I was shocked when several of the most powerful earthquakes ever recorded struck in 2009. I was truly stunned and astounded at the extent of the damage. So I have pondered these things in my heart for several years. This was a sobering experience. Later, on May 6th and May 16th of 2011, the Lord actually had me prophesy that earthquakes would transpire in both Montego Bay and Kingston, Jamaica. (I was ministering in these two cities when the earthquakes transpired.) In both instances significant earthquakes shook the Jamaica within hours of those prophetic words! There is a whole lot of shaking going on!

Here are a few examples of earthquakes that transpired in the following months as recorded by China.org:

Haiti: Haiti was struck by a devastating magnitude 7.0 earthquake...killing up to 230,000 people and affecting millions.

Chile: Chile was ravaged by a magnitude 8.8 earthquake...ranking it the fifth strongest earthquake since 1900. It caused more than 800 deaths in the region. A tsunami alert was waived over all countries of the Pacific Rim.

China: The magnitude 7.1 quake hits Yushu county in north-west China's Qinghai Province..., which killed at least 2,200 people and left more than 100,000 homeless.

Sumatra, Indonesia: A major earthquake with a magnitude of 7.5 strikes off the western coast of Sumatra, Indonesia..., which killed 435 and leaving over 110 missing. The earthquake also triggered a substantial localized tsunami.

Turkey: A magnitude 6.1 earthquake shook eastern Turkey's Elazığ city, and the final death toll was reported at 58, leaving more than 100 injured.

Papua, Indonesia: A 7.0 earthquake struck the coast near Papua, Indonesia..., killing 17 and damaging hundreds of homes.

Baja, California, Mexico: A 7.2 magnitude quake rocks Mexico's Baja California ..., killing two people and causing tremors as far away as Nevada.

Taiwan: A magnitude 6.4 earthquake struck Kaohsiung, Taiwan's southern city..., resulting in more than 90 injuries and minor damage.

New Zealand: A 7.1 magnitude earthquake has rocked New Zealand's second largest city Christchurch, causing widespread damage and at least two people were seriously injured, including the collapse of some buildings [including the Christchurch Cathedral] and power outages.

Japan: Japan's southern Ryukyu Islands, Okinawa, experienced a 7.0 magnitude earthquake.... A Pacific wide tsunami warning went into effect immediately after the earthquake news hit.[1]

I do not believe that it was a coincidence that it was Christ-church that was shaken by the 7.1 magnitude earthquake in New Zealand. There are obvious symbolic and prophetic correlations evident in this episode of God shaking the heavens and the earth.

The prophet Joel spoke of signs and wonders like these in the earth and in the heavens. We see that prophesy in Joel 2:28-32:

And it shall come to pass afterward That I will pour out My Spirit on all flesh; Your sons and your daughters shall prophesy, Your old men shall dream dreams, Your young men shall see visions. And also on My menservants and on My maidservants I will pour out My Spirit in those days. And I will show wonders in the heavens and in the earth: Blood and fire and pillars of smoke. The sun shall be turned into darkness, And the moon into blood, Before the coming of the great and awesome day of the LORD. And it shall come to pass That whoever calls on the name of the LORD Shall be saved. For in Mount Zion and in Jerusalem there shall be deliverance, As the LORD has said, Among the remnant whom the LORD calls.

All of these signs have come to pass in and upon the earth since Yom Kippur 2009.

The shaking the Lord had spoken to me about only increases. However, the Lord is preparing His remnant of people to walk in supernatural peace and protection through all of these shakings and wonders in the heavens and in the earth. God can give you His perfect plans to protect and keep you in this hour. That kind of revelation is an aspect of unlocking the hidden mysteries of the powers of the age to come.

Day of Atonement 2010

In 2010, the moment that I positioned myself to hear the Lord on the Day of Atonement, the Holy Spirit began to pour out notes and scriptures to me and I started to write all of this revelation down. So I want to relate what I heard from the Lord on the Day of Atonement in 2010 because it further illustrates the shaking that is upon us at this hour.

The Lord has impressed upon me the need to proclaim to His people the scriptural principle of the priesthood of all believers (see 1 Peter 2:5, 9). So we have been trumpeting that message since then. I need to make that an obtainable thing for all believers and pre-believers.

Everyone should also take the time to cultivate an intimate relationship with the Holy Spirit, the Father, and the Christ. I need to hear God clearly for myself, and you will need to hear the Lord for yourself as well in the coming days as this shaking increases. It is imperative! After all, that is the true first commandment. We need to cultivate the ability to hear God for ourselves.

On Yom Kippur and The Day of Atonement 2010, the moment that I positioned myself to wait upon the Lord the

Holy Spirit began to speak to me to read Psalms 108 through 112. The Lord has been speaking to me about the priesthood of all believers over the last few years. I believe that we need to come into an understanding and revelation of who (and what) we really are *in Christ*. We are a royal priesthood and a chosen generation.

1 Peter 2:9–10

You are a chosen generation, a royal priesthood, a holy nation, His own special people, that you may proclaim the praises of Him who called you out of darkness into His marvelous light; who once were not a people but are now the people of God, who had not obtained mercy but now have obtained mercy.

We are sons and daughters of the Most High God, and we are citizens of the Kingdom of Light. However, many of us do not understand our true regenerated nature, nor do we have the revelation of the authority that we carry as God's children. The Lord has begun to lead me to trumpet this message. Much of this dynamic of our identity deals with Christ's role and ministry. Jesus ministered in the role or anointing of the royal Priest after the order of Melchizedek.

We are also called to emulate Jesus' example in this royal priesthood according to the order of Melchizedek (1 Peter 2:21; Hebrews 12:1-2; Hebrews 6). (We will look at your calling as a royal priest according to the order of Melchizedek in more detail later in this book.)

The Priesthood of All Believers

Many in the Body of Christ will be empowered to step into the "priesthood of all believers" if they press in at this season. You can be transformed into a mature son or daughter of the Most High God as you learn how simple it is to actually rest in the Lord and access the heavenly dimensions.

One aspect of the priesthood of all believers is an understanding of how to operate in the power of the Holy Spirit by living your life under an open heaven. Another aspect of the priesthood of all believers is realizing that Christ has given us an example to follow and that we are called to be priests after the order of Melchizedek having free access into the realms of heaven. There we will receive supernatural revelation that will empower us to demonstrate Christ's Kingdom with not only the anointing and power of the Holy Spirit but also in the full power of the Trinity. This is yet another attribute of the hidden mysteries of the powers of the age to come.

This is Christ's example for us. An important part of priesthood of all believers is the God-given ability to pass through the heavens, just like Jesus the Son of God, and freely obtain revelation knowledge there and to be empowered by God Almighty.

Hebrews 4:14 further illustrates your role as a royal priest according to the order of Melchizedek: *"Seeing then that we have a great High Priest who has passed through the heavens, Jesus the Son of God, let us hold fast our confession."*

As I studied Psalms 108 through 112 on the Day of Atonement, I realized that this was exactly what I had been hearing for the last few years; and what's more, Holy Spirit pressed upon me to include some of this material in this writing. (I believe that it is a good idea to invest some time doing a word study of Psalms 108 through 112 at this hour, especially Psalm 110.)

Again on the Day of Atonement in 2012 and 2013, the Lord continued to impress upon me the importance of the royal priesthood according to the order of Melchizedek. Really all that means is that we learn to become more like Jesus and minister in the way that He did. We learn to live our lives in a Christlike manner and walk in love and humility. We learn to walk in heavenly authority and supernatural power. God's people need to begin to learn about the anointing or mantle of Melchizedek. The Lord showed me very clearly that the key to becoming a royal priest according to the order of Melchizedek is to be diligent to enter into the rest of the Lord.

A Universal Shaking

I have preached and written about this dynamic extensively over the last few years in many places about how the Lord Jesus had visited me on the Day of Atonement in 2011 and again in 2012. It bears repeating here. Those experiences are well documented in my book *The Sword of the Lord & the Rest of the Lord.* However, as the Lord prepared me for the Day of Atonement in 2013, it seemed that I experienced the culmination of those two powerful visitations once more in the spirit or heavenly realms.

Although God has implemented a universal shaking upon the earth and within the Body of Christ, you need not be alarmed. The shaking of the Lord is really His mercy and will ultimately unfold for the good of those who love the Lord. It will be a Romans 8:28 dynamic: *"We know that all things work together for good to those who love God, to those who are the called according to His purpose."*

The question really becomes, where is your true allegiance? Are you rooted and grounded in the world and its systems? Are you rooted and grounded in a religious system and a form of godliness? Or, are you rooted and grounded on the solid Rock of Jesus Christ? All of these kingdoms will be violently shaken at this season. The real question that you need to ask yourself is where are you standing in the reality and in the Spirit?

Jesus prophesied about perilous times and this kind of shaking that we are experiencing upon the earth today in Matthew 7:24-29. Here is what the Lord said:

> *"Therefore whoever hears these sayings of Mine, and does them, I will liken him to a wise man who built his house on the rock: and the rain descended, the floods came, and the winds blew and beat on that house; and it did not fall, for it was founded on the rock. But everyone who hears these sayings of Mine, and does not do them, will be like a foolish man who built his house on the sand: and the rain descended, the floods came, and the winds blew and beat on that house; and it fell. And great was its fall." And so it was, when Jesus had ended these sayings, that the people were astonished at His teaching, for He taught them as one having authority, and not as the scribes.*

Jesus also prophesied about the shaking the earth is experiencing in Matthew 24:29-31 (emphasis added):

*Immediately after the tribulation of those days the sun will be darkened, and the moon will not give its light; the stars will fall from heaven, and **the powers of the heavens will be shaken**. Then the sign of the Son of Man will appear in heaven, and then all the tribes of the earth will mourn, and they will see **the Son of Man coming on the clouds of heaven with power and great glory**. And He will send His angels with a great sound of a trumpet, and they will gather together His elect from the four winds, from one end of heaven to the other.*

I want to encourage you that the shaking does not have to be a bad thing for you. You can learn to rise above the shaking and this evil age. Again, this is another aspect of the hidden mysteries of the powers of the age to come. Allow me to begin to unlock some of these hidden mysteries that can help you to be transformed into a mature son and daughter of the Most High God. Then you will be empowered to rise above this shaking of the kingdoms of the earth.

CHAPTER 4

Learning to Soar and to Roar

There is an acceleration of the dynamics of Christ's Kingdom advancing and invading the kingdoms of the earth. During the last few weeks leading up to the Day of Atonement this year (2013), there was a real and marked quickening of the manifestation of the Kingdom of Heaven. As the shaking of the church and the world increases, so too shall the Kingdom of Heaven begin to invade the terrestrial or earthly realms at an accelerated rate.

There is a stirring in the spirit. As I was in preparation for the Moravian Falls Heaven Touching Earth Gathering #5 School of the Seers, the Lord opened the heavenly realms dramatically. This acceleration or opening of the heavenly realms is happening much more often and much more easily. In fact, many people are beginning to experience this supernatural dynamic as the Lord is opening the spiritual ears and eyes of His people. God is empowering and enabling His friends to arise above the swirl of this world to be seated far above the powers and principalities of this world that is being so shaken, disturbed, and disrupted. God is pouring out His good treasure the heavens (Deuteronomy 28:12)!

There is a marked acceleration of the heavens becoming much more thin or porous in many different places today. The heavens are invading my sphere of influence on airplanes, in cars, and even in my dreams. Heaven is invading earth. In fact, this phenomenon has become common at the last several Schools of the Seers that we have hosted. At the leading of the Lord, we have hosted regional and international Schools of the Seers in many places since 2007.

The Priesthood of All Believers

These schools are designed to equip God's people to walk in wisdom and maturity. The Schools of the Seers seem to be blessed by the breath of God as miracles, signs, and wonders always follow the preaching of the Gospel of the Kingdom at these King of Glory Ministries International events. The result is that lives are changed and people are empowered to become a little more like Jesus Christ and encouraged to do the same things that Jesus Himself did. Not by me, but by the Spirit of the living God! I want to share the following testimonies as they are pivotal to the unfolding of my understanding and revelation of the powers of the age to come.

At one of the School of the Seers in 2013, we went into another dimension and God did amazing things! The entire gathering of over 300 people was taken into the heavenly dimensions. As a result many experienced the realms of heaven firsthand. Many people had their spiritual eyes and ears opened and began to see and hear from the heavenly dimensions. There was a supernatural impartation of the seer anointing. Dozens of people reported seeing and hearing from the realms of heaven for the first time. Many experienced the heavenly realm with all five of their temporal senses. In other words, they all started to minister unto God the Father as the priesthood of all believers (Revelation 1:5-6).

In several sessions the angels of God were heard singing in unison with the spontaneous worship in the meetings. Many saw the Lord Jesus Christ step into the meetings. Others saw members of the great cloud of witnesses. Still others saw and recognized the Lord's angels. Others saw unusual angelic beings or members of the Lord's angelic hosts. People reported smelling the fragrances of heaven. The smell of frankincense, myrrh, and roses were manifested. The fragrance of the Lord permeated the conference center. We experienced an unusual amount and outpouring of miracles, signs, and wonders in the venue.

At times people actually felt attributes of the heavenly realms with their sense of touch. Others began to actually taste honey and other flavors of the Kingdom of Heaven as heaven literally invaded earth at the School of the Seers. People heard the voices of the angels of heaven entering into the worship at the meetings with their ears. All of these manifestations are attributes of the royal priesthood according to the order of Melchizedek. Before one of our School of the Seers, I experienced a powerful visitation of heaven. I want to share this prophetic experience with you because I believe that it is actually a prophetic word that can help you to rise above the shaking and turbulence of the world in your sphere of influence at this hour. This is a valid word for you at this hour *if you can receive it!*

Learn to Soar and Roar

August 28, 2012, at 7:38, as I was waiting in prayer seeking the Lord for the School of the Seers, I was taken up into the heavenly realms. I came to a place that I had been before, the sea of glass like crystal. On Tuesday, May 28, 2002, I had been in the Talapia Hotel in Mwanza, Tanzania, when the heavens opened and I fell upon this same place. I had landed on the seashore of the sea of glass like crystal, and there the Lord Jesus had come to me and began to teach me about the "seer anointing." I will share more about this later.

This morning I was not lying upon the shore, which is made up of rubies, diamonds, sapphires, and other precious stones, but I was standing upon the shore. I was gazing out at the crystal clear waters for a moment, when the celestial sun rose upon the sea of glass like crystal and with it an explosion of supernatural colors. This was an arising of the glory of God and not what we understand or perceive as the sun with our carnal or temporal minds. This was not the sun like we see at the center of our solar system. This was a supernatural sun. This was a heavenly Son.

This was actually the Son of Righteousness arising with healing in His wings (Malachi 4:2; Isaiah 60)! These amazing colors released a spectacular light show that began to dance upon the perfectly still waters and reflect the tangible glory of God with this marvelous plethora of colors between the sky and the sea. I watched this for a few moments, and I had a knowing that the Lord had brought me to the sea of glass like crystal for a purpose. As this thought came into my mind, a spiritual being began to buzz back and forth in front of my eyes.

I had seen spiritual beings like this before around the Father's throne in the heavenly realms. I believe it was a seraph, and it was moving supernaturally fast. I could see its wings moving in sweeping circles which seemed to disperse the very glory of God in all directions. I gazed at this seraph as it flew around me for several moments. The sounds of its wings were amazing and very loud. It seemed to be about the dimensions of a human-sized hummingbird as it moved acrobatically in the air around me. It was difficult to see it clearly because it moved so fast that it appeared to be a blur of colors and glory.

Suddenly this seraph flew directly in front of my eyes and stopped for an instant. At that moment I saw the head of a golden lion. The lion roared, and the force of the roar seemed to send the hair on my head flying back like a strong wind. The roar of the lion head was very loud and very clear! I thought about this for a moment, and the seraph returned and flew directly in front of my eyes a second time. When this seraph stopped again, it revealed the head of an eagle.

The eagle was not a bald eagle but a golden eagle. The golden eagle lingered a little longer in front of me and gazed into my eyes for a moment. I saw this magnificent creature's pupils dilate as it seemed to gaze into the windows of my soul. Instantly I remembered what the Lord has taught me about the golden eagle. Golden eagles represent the seer anointing, which is a prophetic anointing of the mature believer in Christ. The golden eagle, in my opinion, represents the mature sons and daughters of the Most High God. As this thought entered into my mind, the face of the golden eagle screeched and the seraph zoomed up into the heavenly realms dispersing the glory of God as he went!

Suddenly I felt someone tap me on the right shoulder. When I turned around I saw Jesus standing there smiling at me and looking at me with His beautiful eyes. His countenance exuded the love of God. Then the Lord spoke to me saying:

> The time has come for My people to arise. They will prophesy what they see. They shall roar like a golden lion. They will shriek like a golden eagle. When this happens the enemy will flee. Tell them the time has come to roar like a lion and to soar like an eagle, soaring the highest heights of the heavenly realms where they will rise up above the confusion and conflicts of the world. From that place they will overcome the world and enter into My perfect will and the fullness of My rest. Tell them to soar into the heavenly realms and see what must take place after this.

The Lord is still telling His people to soar and to roar!

The Lord is still telling His people to rest and to confess!

A Passion for Christ

Acts 4:19-20 is scriptural promise for you today: *"Peter and John answered and said to them, 'Whether it is right in the sight of God to listen to you more than to God, you judge. For we cannot but speak the things which we have seen and heard.'"*

Here is promise for those of you reading this with a hungry heart and a passion for Christ. The God of the universe is calling you to see and hear. He is calling you to speak of those things that you discern from the heavenly realms! Then, like Peter and John, you will decree: "For we cannot but speak the things which we have seen and heard."

The Lord is calling you to Revelations 4:1; in fact, this is a promise for you at this day and at this hour. This is a promise for those of you who are reading this right now! "*After these things I looked, and behold, a door standing open in heaven. And the first voice which I heard was like a trumpet speaking with me, saying, 'Come up here, and I will show you things which must take place after this.'*"

For many of you the Lord is opening the heavenly realms in your life. You are not reading this book by accident! For many of you this book will be your Mahanaim, or camp of God. It will be the place where your spiritual ears and eyes are opened to see and to hear from God clearly. God will begin to speak to you as a man speaks to a friend. You will become like Jacob in Genesis 32:2: "*When Jacob saw the angels of God, he said, 'This is God's camp.' And he called the name of that place Mahanaim.*"

No matter where you are reading this today, you are in the right place at the right time. You have become geographically and chronologically obedient, and the Lord is going to reward you and pour out His blessing and His grace upon you.

A Door Is Opened in Heaven

I believe that there is truly a door that has been opened in the heavenly realms. It is possible that this door was not available

35

to us before this hour. We have entered into a *kairos* moment of time upon God's supernatural calendar. The Lord is opening the heavens and inviting you to "come up here"! The God of the universe is seeking to reveal to you hidden and mysterious things from the secret places of the Kingdom of Heaven.

God is seeking to show you things that must take place after this!

I am describing your role as a royal priest according to the order of Melchizedek. You can access the heavenly dimensions and receive hidden revelation and manna from the Kingdom of Heaven. You can learn to discern the things that *MUST* take place after this. What we are speaking of is a Kingdom of Heaven dynamic.

It is only possible because of the day and the hour in which we live. It is only possible because of the supernatural exchange that the Messiah released at the Cross of Calvary and through His victorious resurrection from the dead. I am speaking of your role as a royal priest according to the order of Melchizedek. You can see this supernatural dynamic outlined in Revelation 1:5-6:

> *Jesus Christ, the faithful witness, the firstborn from the dead, and the ruler over the kings of the earth. To Him who loved us and washed us from our sins in His own blood, and has made us kings and priests to His God and Father, to Him be glory and dominion forever and ever. Amen.*

The Mantle of Melchizedek

What we see here is the love of God, or what I like to refer to as the Apostolic Love of Christ. The love of Jesus makes us righteous and holy to minister to our God and Father. We are called to minister as priests and prophets (as the Spirit wills). You are called to minister in the kingly anointing. You are called to minister as a royal priest according to the order of Melchizedek. I will write about this dynamic of the powers of the age to come in much more detail later. But what does that mean? It means that you will walk in the seer realms and will have the gift of discerning of spirits activated in your life. You will walk in great power and authority. We are talking about becoming an overcomer!

We see this outlined in Revelation 3:21-22: "*To him who overcomes I will grant to sit with Me on My throne, as I also overcame and sat down with My Father on His throne. 'He who has an ear, let him hear what the Spirit says to the churches.'*"

We are born to grow and to mature into the very image of Christ. We are designed to have our minds renewed and transformed into "Christlike minds." We are talking about being transformed into Christlike character. This is an important key to understanding and entering into the mantle of Melchizedek.

We must also understand the rest of the Lord. Entering into the rest of the Lord is perhaps the most important key to activating the Lord's spiritual DNA in your life. I call that waiting or resting prayer. I refer to this dynamic of God's glory as transformation glory. Transformation glory empowers you to develop this kind of supernatural prayer life. It is different than intercession. You are no longer praying on earth directing your words up to heaven. Rather, you are praying from the heavenly realms and releasing powerful God inspired decrees down upon the earth like supernatural missiles. In other words, you begin to minister according to the royal priesthood according to the order of Melchizedek. You enter into the priesthood of all believers. This, too, is one of the hidden mysteries of the powers of the age to come.

Hebrews 12:2 describes this: "*Looking unto Jesus, the author and finisher of our faith, who for the joy that was set before Him endured the cross, despising the shame, and has sat down at the right hand of the throne of God.*"

And again, this scripture confirms that through Christ's finished work upon Calvary, He was and is seated by the Father's right hand of power and authority as prophesied in Psalm 110. We have been given this same freedom and access to God's throne of grace and power through the Atonement. We *can* sit with God in heavenly places today.

This promise is found in Ephesians 1:3: "*Blessed be the God and Father of our Lord Jesus Christ, who has blessed us with every spiritual blessing in the heavenly places.*" Ephesians 2:6 also illustrates this promise that you have from the Lord that God "*raised us up together, and made us sit together in the heavenly places in Christ Jesus.*"

Looking at Psalm 110 verse 1 we are told the fruit of being seated at the very right hand of God: "*Till I make Your enemies Your footstool.*" This is a beautiful portrait of the royal priesthood after the order of Melchizedek. God will conquer and vanquish our enemies on our behalf! You rise above the shakings of the world and enter into the realms and rest of heaven. Again, I encourage you to study Psalm 110 in depth.

Not only that, the Father will place our enemies under our feet. The truth is that our total triumph and victory over our foes is already finished. The enemy of our soul is already defeated and is, in fact, under our feet. We just need to get the revelation of this fact, and then we need to begin to walk it out in the temporal or earthly realm. We can be enlightened and empowered to possess the gates of our enemies.

An important key to this is just realizing that we have the liberty to access the heavenly places and obtain God's revelation, power, and delegated authority. We need to learn to be led by our renewed or reborn spirit and not our unregenerate minds and flesh. I believe that this kind of power and authority is available to anyone at this hour. Now, Praise God, we can get our minds renewed by the word of God. Amen! In the next chapter I want to look at what I refer to as "the whosoever anointing."

CHAPTER 5

The Whosoever Anointing

As this unending season of shaking accelerates and continues, God will begin to raise up a Caleb generation. These people will become forerunners in the spirit. They will learn to step into or through the open heavens and see the things that the Lord is showing them that must take place after this! I do not believe that these marvelous and amazing gifts that the Father is releasing are exclusively for the "chosen vessel" any longer. This is my opinion.

The Caleb generation will see and hear well from the heavenly realms. They will say, "We are well able!" They will learn to go where no man has gone before! Even as Caleb was willing and ready to go and conquer the Promised Land, these overcomers will conquer the heavenly realms. Let's search out this spiritual dynamic.

Look at Numbers 13:30: *"Then Caleb quieted the people before Moses, and said, 'Let us go up at once and take possession, for **we are well able to overcome it**'"* (emphasis added). We see the whosoever anointing, or what some call the Caleb anointing, in the book of Joshua. Many in this hour (those who are mature in years, yet renewed and young in the spirit) will see and decree the heart of God concerning their Christ-ordained destinies and spiritual DNA.

Joshua 14:7-13

I was forty years old when Moses the servant of the LORD sent me from Kadesh Barnea to spy out the land, and I brought back word to him as it was in my heart. Nevertheless my brethren who went up with me made the heart of the people melt, but I wholly followed the LORD my God. So Moses swore on that day, saying, "Surely the land where your foot has trodden shall be your inheritance and your children's forever, because you have wholly followed the LORD my God." And now, behold, the LORD has kept me alive, as He said, these forty-five years, ever since the LORD spoke this word to Moses while Israel wandered in the wilderness; and now, here I am this day, eighty-five years old. As yet I am as strong this day as on the day that Moses sent me; just as my strength was then, so now is my strength for war, both for going out and for coming in. Now therefore, give me this mountain of which the LORD spoke in that day; for you heard in that day how the Anakim were there, and that the cities were great and fortified. It may be that the LORD will be with me, and I shall be able to drive them out as the LORD said. And Joshua [A type of royal priest according to the order of Melchizedek] *blessed him, and gave Hebron to Caleb the son of Jephunneh as an inheritance.*

Not all who will walk in this type of anointing and power will be of the Joshua generation. Some will be of the Caleb generation. We need both. The army of God that is being assembled at this hour will be comprised of both the young and the young at heart. God will raise up an end-time army from the ages of two to eighty-two and beyond. These mighty ones will walk in the power and authority of heaven!

You could call this the mantle of the royal priesthood after the order of Melchizedek. It is a precious thing which the Father sent His only Son to establish upon the earth. In essence, we are speaking about a God-ordained or *kairos* moment of time when the Lord will freely give His power to His friends.

It is a set time, and an army of God will be cloaked in holiness. They will be anointed with dew of youth. Their chronological age will not matter, and many will do great and mighty exploits for the Kingdom of Heaven. They will experience a rebirth of the spirit. Or, as Jesus actually said, there will be a set time when Christ's people will be born from above or born from the realms of heaven (John 3:3). That day is at hand!

This anointing is for both the young and the old. Yes, there will be a great move of God and mass salvations among the youth. But there will also be a "Caleb anointing" that will come upon the "mature Body of Christ." They will say, "We are well able."

Supernatural Forerunners

I am speaking of a rebirth of your spirit, soul, and body. Yes, our spirit is renewed at the moment of salvation, but we need a transformation of our soul and our flesh.

I am referring to an army, or chosen tribe of God's champions, who will be given free access to ascend through the open heavens (access that Christ has restored to mankind) to sit at the right hand of God in holiness, kingly authority, and supernatural power. God will raise up a generation of spiritual fathers who will be empowered by the Spirit of the living God to train and equip His people to be transformed into mature sons and daughters of God. Many of these people will be of the Caleb generation. They will minister in the anointing and grace of the royal priesthood according to the order of Melchizedek. These supernatural forerunners will father and equip the next generation in these supernatural realities.

Psalm 110:4 summarizes this promise and the definition of this free gift from our Father: "*The LORD has sworn And will not relent, 'You are a priest forever According to the order of Melchizedek.'*" What a promise the Father has given to you! You are called to be a royal priest after the order of Melchizedek who will rule and reign with the power and authority of the Father's throne. These dynamics are manifesting upon the earth today and are accelerating at a rapid pace. Christ has given us an example to emulate.

Christ has anointed you to rule and reign upon the earth as a priest and prophet (as the Spirit wills). Allow me to clarify this statement by saying that not all of you who touch this heavenly calling will sit in the office of the prophet. However, scripture clearly states that we can all prophesy according to the level of our faith (Romans 12:6; 1 Corinthians 14:24, 26; Acts 2:17). Don't go and get religious on me, OK? The Lord is calling you to be a king with dominion power and authority upon the earth at this hour. It is possible for you to speak to the storms and command them to be still. It is possible for you to decree earthquakes and other phenomenon and watch them come to pass upon the earth quickly. It is possible for you to grow into the character and image of Jesus and take authority over spiritual gates of darkness and rule in your sphere of influence with Kingdom power and with God's delegated supernatural authority. Again, these are all attributes of the hidden mysteries of the powers of the age to come.

You were created to be a royal priest that will extend the dominion of Christ's Kingdom. You were created to extend the dominion of Christ's Kingdom as a royal priesthood after the order of Melchizedek who will rule and reign with the power and authority of heaven upon the earth. The power of heaven shall back up your words.

Zechariah 6:12-13 also paints a portrait of this role of Christ:

Thus says the LORD of hosts, saying: "Behold, the Man whose name is the BRANCH! From His place He shall branch out, And He shall build the temple of the LORD; Yes, He shall build the temple of the LORD. He shall bear the glory, And shall sit and rule on His throne; So He shall be a priest on His throne, And the counsel of peace shall be between them both."

Royal Priests Around the Throne

In my opinion, this refers to Christ and His Bride ministering as mediators between the heavenly realm and the temporal or earthly realm. Again, this is yet another facet of the royal priesthood after the order of Melchizedek—to rule and reign with the delegated power of God's throne of mercy and grace.

This last passage also refers to "both" Gentile and Jewish believers in Jesus who will be reunited into one spotless bride before the return of the Messiah.

We are all called (all of God's people) to be priests around or before the throne.

This speaks of entering into the fullness of the rest of the Lord and allowing God to work on our behalf. We rest in the Lord and the Lord rests upon us, and He does the greater works in our life and in our sphere of influence. We learn to minister and live from a place of peace and rest.

When we can begin to understand our high calling as a priest after the order of Melchizedek, we can begin to enter into the heavenly realms. Then we will begin to see God Almighty fight on our behalf. There are not many people who have ever tapped into this kind of heavenly power and authority. Those who have were all extremely close friends of God.

Some of the people in the Bible who walked in this kind of authority were Moses, Elijah, Enoch, and, of course, Christ. They are all examples of people who operated in the anointing of the mantle of Melchizedek.

Missions of Mercy

These friends of God were not always subject to the laws of nature; and miracles, signs, and wonders were normal for them. Of course, they were just human beings like you and me. In the coming days there will be times that regular people will be given a similar power and dominion over the laws of nature.

I once had a brief opportunity to speak to Bob Jones about this dynamic, and he called people like this "mercynaries."

This supernatural authority may be given from God to His friends periodically to fulfill a mandate or missions of mercy. God is preparing a tribe of friends that will not always be subject to the laws of nature at certain God-ordained moments of time; and extraordinary miracles, signs, and wonders will be normal for them too. This, too, is an aspect of the hidden mysteries of the powers of the age to come.

These people may not walk in this level of God-given authority constantly, but at times this mantle of Melchizedek will come upon them to release great (mega, *dunamis*) signs and wonders in the name of Jesus. They will walk in the anointing of a priest and prophet (as the Holy Spirit wills) according to the order or mantle of Melchizedek. They will have revelation and understanding of the hidden mysteries of the powers of the age to come. What is more, God will give them the delegated authority to minister and live in this incredible power and amazing supernatural revelations as He wills. What an amazing time to be alive!

Supernatural authority, signs, wonders, and miracles will be common for these friends of the living God. You are called to walk in this kind of God-ordained intimacy and power too.

That is exactly what God wants for you and me today. The Lord is calling us to "come up here" into the heavenly realms and to see and hear what must take place after this.

Revelation 4:1 is the hour that we are living in today. We can have free access to the very throne of God. This is the promise and cry of the Lord's heart at this hour: *"Come up here, and I will* *show you things which must take place after this"* (emphasis added).

In the next chapter we will continue to unlock some of the hidden mysteries of the powers of the age to come. Let's look at how it is possible for you to boldly come before the throne of mercy and grace and access the heavenly dimensions to impact the earthly realm in your sphere of influence for God's glory and for His Kingdom.

CHAPTER 6

Mature Sons and Daughters of the Most High God, Arise!

Heaven will continue to invade earth. This too will also accelerate in the coming season. Some people will not know how to handle these supernatural invasions of their time and space by the God of the universe. However, there will be a remnant of mature sons and daughters of the Most High God who will welcome such divine interruptions with zeal and passion. Many of these friends of God will begin to walk in a much greater level of wisdom and revelation. They will learn to entertain heaven upon earth. It would be good for you to understand that many of these anointed ones will not fit into the mold or pattern that you might be expecting. God will raise up the most unlikely and will begin to release suddenlies into the earth to proclaim His message and His Kingdom with His power and authority. These mature sons and daughters will come from every walk of life and from every denomination.

Get ready! These manifestations of the Kingdom of God will not be in word alone (powerless, fleshly prophesy and preaching) but in unusual demonstrations of the power of God confirmed by miracles, signs and wonders, and manifestations of the Kingdom of Heaven. The Lord will begin to release unusual people from His Kingdom who will operate in unusual levels of Kingdom authority with amazing signs and wonders following their preaching and daily lives. These mature sons and daughters of God will preach the Gospel of the Kingdom at all times. They will preach the Gospel of the Kingdom everywhere they go; and at times they *may* actually use words. These *arising* ones will become living epistles of the Most High God (2 Corinthians 3:2-3).

In fact, there will be a great acceleration of the manifestations of the Kingdom of God in the lives and ministries of those who truly love the Lord and are called according to His purposes. The Lord will continue to hasten the release of His Kingdom in the days to come. Signs and wonders will mark the mature sons and daughters of God in the coming days as the shaking increases. In all things these living epistles will be more than conquerors through Christ.

There will be more wisdom and understanding concerning the hidden mysteries and revelatory knowledge of Christ's Kingdom. The Lord will hasten His people's ability to discover the secrets locked within the Canon of Scripture. He will also help His people discover spiritual truths concerning the Kingdom of Heaven and their ability and authority to access the heavenly realms to tap into and access the power(s) of God to be discerned there.

This will accelerate as the Lord helps people exercise their spiritual senses by reason of use as outlined in Hebrews 5:14: *"Solid food belongs to those who are of full age, that is, those who by reason of use have their senses exercised to discern both good and evil."*

Released to Recognize

These mature sons and daughters will grow in knowledge and understanding of the realms of the spiritual Kingdom that our God created and inhabits. The "solid food" described in this scripture could also be translated as the "hidden or mysterious" secrets of the Kingdom of God.

It is surely the glory of God to conceal a matter or secret, but it is the glory of kings to search these hidden heavenly treasures out. We see this dynamic outlined in Proverbs 25:2: *"It is the glory of God to conceal* [hide, keep covered, or to conceal] *a matter* [power, hidden promise, or supernatural provision], *But the glory of kings is to search out* [unearth, uncover a hidden object of value, or discover] *a matter."*

There are hidden promises and concealed treasure in Christ's Kingdom that the Lord has held back for such a time as this. There are spiritual dynamics and attributes in the Kingdom of Heaven that we can dig out, search out, and discover. In fact, it gives the Father great pleasure to give you the Kingdom of Heaven. Luke 12:32 makes this fact perfectly clear: *"Do not fear, little flock, for it is your Father's good pleasure to give you the kingdom."*

As we learn to develop our spiritual senses, we can grow and mature in our spiritual discernment. As our discernment becomes mature and we become mature sons and daughters of God, at times we will be released to recognize the hidden mysteries of the Kingdom of Heaven. One of the supernatural dynamics that is accelerating at this hour is the release and manifestation of open heavens, or spiritual gates, in our meetings and in our sphere of influence.

When these spiritual gates or doors open, there is access between the heavenly dimensions and the earthly dimensions. At times like this we can see and hear what the Father is doing. Then, like Christ, we will do those things that we see our Father doing in the same manner that Jesus described in John 5:19: *"The Son can do nothing of Himself, but what He sees the Father do; for whatever He does, the Son also does in like manner."*

Jesus saw what the Father was doing because He was a seer. God is calling you to be a seer too. At times you will begin to see or discern spiritual gates or open heavens that manifest in your life. These gates or open heavens are recorded throughout the Bible. So these supernatural gates or windows of heaven are quite well documented and accepted in the Canon of Scripture. We see one prominent example in Genesis 32:2: *"When Jacob saw them* [God's angels], *he said, 'This is God's camp.' And he called the name of that place Mahanaim."* God is opening the heavens to many people at this hour, and this phenomenon will only increase in the days ahead.

This is really the fruit of the acceleration of the gift of discerning of spirits, or what some people call the gift of discernment. More and more people will be given the grace and the anointing or God-given ability to discern or see spiritual gates or portals of glory as they begin to manifest and invade our space as the return of Christ draws near. By the way, you don't always have to see spiritual gates with your eyes to discern their presence and availability. I call this grace gift the seer anointing. In my opinion, the seer anointing is another aspect of the hidden and mysterious secrets of the powers of the age to come. I am not digging into this dynamic of the Kingdom (the seer anointing) in this book, but I have written extensively about the seer anointing and how you can access this gift from the Lord in my trilogy on the seer anointing.

Accessing the Heavenly Dimensions

Recently I have begun to experience an interesting phenomenon. At times the Lord is taking me into other dimensions. Personally I believe that this is an extension or attribute of the seer anointing and a dynamic of the powers of the age to come. On Wednesday, August 28, 2013, I had another experience of being transported into the heavenly dimensions. Although I am not positive, it is possible that I was also transported or translated in the natural realm as well.

I had driven to Greensboro, North Carolina, to pick up my friend Paul Cox. Paul was arriving on American Airlines flight 3358 from Dallas, Texas. He was coming to speak at the upcoming Heaven Touching Earth Gathering #5 School of the Seers. He arrived near midnight. We picked up some snacks and milk, and off into the blissful North Carolina night we went.

Shortly, as we were driving along, it seemed as if the whole atmosphere around us shifted. We seemed to be translated and a "spiritual bubble" appeared to encircle the car we were traveling in. The glory of God invaded our space, and we were both aware that we "were not alone." The heavens opened around us. We believe that a Godly spiritual being that we discerned to be "the spirit of prophesy" visited us, and we became lost in time and space for a period of time. During this interlude the power and glory of the Lord flooded into our location.

We both became filled with the Spirit of God; and that was great, as it was well past midnight by now. Time and space seemed to morph or wrap around us in a peculiar way. It seemed that we were not where we were supposed to be. I believe that we were taken into another dimension—a Godly dimension. In this spiritual bubble we were refreshed and empowered by the Spirit of God. We were refreshed and given revelation concerning the upcoming ministry at the School of the Seers through the ministry of "the spirit of prophesy." As it turned out, this encounter later proved to be very significant to the upcoming School of the Seers and to my personal understanding of the hidden mysteries of the powers of the age to come. In fact, this encounter actually helped birth this book!

This "spiritual bubble" surrounded us for about twenty or thirty minutes. During this time it seemed that the car was driving itself; and I felt that if I would have taken my hands off of the steering wheel that the Toyota would have, in fact, driven itself! When we felt the Kingdom of Heaven lift and the spiritual bubble or heavenly realm lift off of us, I was shocked to realize that we had been translated. I am not positive, as it is possible that we drove to the location we found ourselves. However, I believe that we may have been lifted up in the Spirit and moved about sixty or seventy-five miles to the southeast. We found ourselves in another county.

This experience was somewhat unsettling. Fortunately Paul had a GPS on his smart phone and we were able to navigate our way to Moravian Falls by traveling over back roads. Later

Paul and I agreed that the Lord had indeed moved us geographically in order to protect us from some harm or danger. We gave Him glory for this and arrived in Moravian Falls about thirty-five or forty minutes earlier than should have been possible considering the distance that we needed to travel from Greensboro International Airport (PTI).

Godly Dimensions

After I dropped Paul at the Holyday Inn Express, I pondered these things in my heart. As I was driving to our little cabin, the same power and glory of God filled the rental car and I was off into another "spiritual bubble" of God's glory and grace. I returned home and immediately sought the Lord in my prayer closet. Through revelation I understood that we had and were going to experience "the first fruits" of this kind of spiritual portals or gates into Godly dimensions. These things were going to occur as we moved forward into the School of the Seers. In fact, we were not disappointed!

On Saturday, as Paul and I were praying, a spiritual door or heavenly gate opened in the hotel room. We both discerned that we had the privilege to step into the Godly dimensions through this opening or gate. Together we opened this hidden double door. It was an ancient door, and as we walked through we stepped into a hidden room full of treasure and keys. We stepped into a secret place. We experienced a hidden place in the Kingdom of God. It was a Godly dimension and a Godly place (a secret place) in the heavenly places (Ephesians 1:3) that was hidden in plain sight. I will look at this in more detail later in this book.

The room was one of several in a hallway which was made up of old stones, like one might expect to see in an ancient castle. We found a key ring that opened the ancient door on our right. Entering we found the room full of treasure, and there were many rings of keys hanging on wooden pegs around the perimeter of this ancient secret room. We each understood that we could take some of the keys and the bags of treasure that were stored on the floor of this room. So we did. By revelation we understood that these keys would unlock doors in the spiritual realm, doors to heavenly or Godly dimensions. As a result we believed that there would be manifestations of God's goodness and outpourings of God's supernatural provision in our lives and in the ministry. In fact, both of these ideas and revelations have proven to be quite true. I put my keys on my belt or sash, and Paul also handed me branches from the trees that were growing by the river of life. I placed those into my quiver upon my back. Later we discerned that we had stepped into Isaiah 45.

In the next chapter I will touch on the manifestation of the true sons and daughters of the Most High God. This is the season that the Lord is raising up mature sons and daughters who will embrace the invasions of the heavenly realms into their lives and sphere of influence. Heavenly invasions like I just described await you! Are you ready? I will also explore some revelation about these kind spiritual gates and how you can access the heavenly dimensions for yourself to obtain heavenly blessings (Ephesians 3:1-9). Again this supernatural dynamic is an aspect of the hidden mysteries of the powers of the age to come.

The revelation given to me in the next chapter came as I experienced a supernatural visitation of the heavenly realms in Moravian Falls, North Carolina, as I was writing in my office. The heavenly realms opened and revelation glory came down! Perhaps this was another visitation of the spirit of prophesy?

CHAPTER 7

Accessing the Heavenly Places

In the subsequent chapters I want to review some of the materials and revelations that I included in the book *Unlocking the Hidden Mysteries of the Seer Anointing II: The Blessings of Psalm 24*. I hope to augment those revelations and develop more fully the hidden mysteries and keys from the previous book. In addition to this, the concepts outlined will help you to more fully understand and grasp the hidden mysteries of the powers of the age to come. Hence, I feel that this material is crucial to understanding the crux of this book. I believe that you can take what is written as a prophetic promise for yourself or for your region as you read this chapter. In fact, you can choose to treat the whole book as a promise for you according to the spiritual principle of Revelation 19:10: "*For the testimony of Jesus is the spirit of prophecy.*"

As I was waiting in prayer for this part of the book, I felt as if the Lord breathed upon these passages of scripture to share with you in this book. In fact, as I was working on this I had an encounter with the Holy Spirit. The windows of heaven opened in my office and the realms of heaven invaded my space at the new iMAEC (International Ministry Apostolic Equipping Center). The iMAEC is the home base of The Moravian Falls School of Higher Learning. It was in that atmosphere of glory and of heaven that the Holy Spirit quickened my understanding and released wisdom and revelation from of Isaiah 45:1-8:

> *Thus says the LORD to His anointed, To Cyrus, whose right hand I have held—To subdue nations before him And loose the armor of kings, To open before him the double doors, So that the gates will not be shut: "I will go before you And make the crooked places straight; I will break in pieces the gates of bronze And cut the bars of iron. I will give you the treasures of darkness And hidden riches of secret places, That you may know that I, the LORD, Who call you by your name, Am the God of Israel. For Jacob My servant's sake, And Israel My elect, I have even called you by your name; I have named you, though you have not known Me. I am the LORD, and there is no other; There is no God besides Me. I will gird you, though you have not known Me, That they may know from the rising of the sun to its setting That there is none besides Me. I am the LORD, and there is no other; I form the light and create darkness, I make peace and create calamity; I, the LORD, do all these things." Rain down, you heavens, from above, And let the skies pour down righteousness; Let the earth open, let them bring forth salvation, And let righteousness spring up together. I, the LORD, have created it.*

I believe this is the season that we are in. It's the season of Deuteronomy 28:12 where God is releasing to His people His good treasure of the open heavens. And when God opens the heavens over our lives, the blessings of the heavenly realms, the blessings of Jehovah, rain down upon us. I believe it's the season of the latter rain. I believe it's the season of the fresh rain. I believe that we have stepped into a time when God is going to open up gates, doors, and windows of heaven and that there are going to be blessings poured out upon our lives. I believe some of the things I'm going to share with you were not available a year ago or even two months ago. I believe this is a new thing the Lord is doing. These things are some of the hidden mysteries of the powers of the age to come.

Let's focus on this powerful and timely passage of Scripture. Isaiah 45:1: *"Thus says the LORD."* "Lord" in this passage means Jehovah, Father, God Almighty. The verse continues: *"To His anointed."* The word translated "anointed" is a Hebrew word that is the root word for Messiah. Usually it means a consecrated person, a king, a priest, or a saint. (I believe we are living in a day and an hour that God is raising up a royal priesthood according to the order of Melchizedek spoken of in Hebrews 7:17. I believe we are all called to be transformed into the image of Jesus; we are *all* called to be God's anointed.)

Isaiah 45:1 continues to describe this anointed one which God the Father is addressing: *"To Cyrus, whose right hand I have held."* This is a Hebraism. To hold the right hand, to hold the leg, or to hold the eye of a person means to be held in a position of security by one who is stronger or who has more power or is more powerful or by one who is more skillful in battle than you are. It means to be held or helped by the right hand of God. It means to rest in the Lord and allow Him to work upon your behalf or to hold your right hand. Mothers and fathers have experienced times when your children were toddlers and you held them by their hand as they are learning to walk. That is a picture of what the prophet Isaiah is speaking about in this passage of Scripture.

When we allow God to hold our hand, we are really allowing God to lead us as if we were that small child. This is not a posture of weakness; this is a posture of submission—a meekness that is in no way weakness. This is a posture of rest and trust in the Lord, and it is desirable. When we submit to God and allow Him to hold our right hand, we are meek in the way Jesus referred to in Matthew 5:5: *"Blessed are the meek, For they shall inherit the earth."* It is sometimes interpreted as being weak, but that is not what the Lord meant. It means to be humble, to be spiritually pure, or to be God-minded.

So when we submit to God and allow Him to hold our right hand, we are becoming more Christlike. Our mind is being transformed into the mind of Christ. It means to allow Jehovah to hold our right hand. It speaks of resting in God and allowing the Lord God Almighty, the Lord of Israel—Jehovah, to battle on our behalf. We rest in God and then the Lord works. We rest, God works. When Jesus cried out on the Cross, *"It is finished!"* (John 19:30), His work was done. The Lord no longer labors. He is seated at the right hand of the Father. He has entered into the rest of the Lord that we see in Hebrews 4. That is the message that I am carrying for the Body of Christ and the world today. God is calling His people to quit laboring and to be diligent to enter into His rest (Hebrews 4:11). God is calling His friends to enter into His rest found in the heavenly dimensions at this hour. From that place of rest, God will work on our behalf. That is what this passage of scripture in Isaiah 45 is describing.

An Anointing to Open Up Spiritual Gates

We see next in Isaiah 45:1 that God begins to war on our behalf. We see this dynamic outlined for us: "*To subdue nations before him And loose the armor of kings.*" The language here has a specific meaning. It means the loins or the riches of kings. The Hebrew word translated "kings" is *melekh*. I have encouraged you that God is calling you to be transformed into a royal priest according to the order of Melchizedek by the Spirit and power of Lord (Zechariah 4:6). Melchizedek was the king of peace or the king of Salem. When we begin to realize our God-ordained destiny to step into this type of royal priesthood to become kings and priests or queens and priestesses according to the order of Melchizedek, it's not some farfetched theology. Simply, what it means is that we become transformed into the very image of Jesus.

Jesus Christ is our role model for this type of kingly anointing. It's an anointing to open up spiritual gates and spiritual doors. At certain ordained times God will allow and empower us to step through spiritual gates to release breakthroughs from the heavenly realms into our lives in the natural realm. By reading this you can access this blessing of Jehovah. This is the same dynamic that I described in the last chapter concerning Paul Cox and our supernatural experience of being translated geographically and later accessing the spiritual dimensions of the heavenly places. These kinds of supernatural blessings are often accessed through spiritual doors and gates.

When the scripture says *"the armor of kings"* in Isaiah 45:1, it is speaking of fortified doors, heavily fortified doors at the place where kings had storehouses of riches and treasures. God wants to give those to you. Let's look at this dynamic in a little bit more detail in the Book of Hebrews. Beginning with verse 14 of Hebrews 4, the writer is speaking of allowing God to work on our behalf as we learn to rest in Him: *"Seeing then that we have a great High Priest who has passed through the heavens."* The great High Priest accessed the doors or gates of heaven; He went behind the veil. "Behind the veil" is another Hebraism, which means to enter into the very presence or glory of God or literally into heaven. Jesus passed through the heavens and you can too. Entering into the heavenly places is also accessed through spiritual doors and gates.

Discerning Destiny

Going on with verse 14, we read, *"Jesus the Son of God, let us hold fast our confession."* Praise God, we have a confession we can hold fast to. What is it? Number one, it is impossible for God to lie to us. And number 2, we have a Forerunner who is Jesus Christ of Nazareth, who has entered into the heavenly realms, who has filled the messianic prophesies, who has overcome the world, and who has sat down at the right hand of the Father where He is now resting from His work. We are to emulate that character of Christ; we are to emulate Jesus in this regard at this hour. We are to cease from our works. We are to allow Jehovah to hold our hand and work on our behalf. Then we see and hear from the heavenly realms (discern) the destiny that God has ordained for us to walk in and it unfolds in a supernatural fashion. Our lives and ministries become fashioned after a heavenly pattern (Exodus 25:40).

Scripture speaks of this dynamic in Hebrews 6:17-18:

> *Thus God, determining to show more abundantly to the heirs of promise the immutability of His counsel, confirmed it by an oath, that by two immutable things, in which it is impossible for God to lie, we might have strong consolation, who have fled for refuge to lay hold of the hope set before us.*

What hope do we have? Scripture tells us as we go on to verses 19: "*This hope we have as an anchor of the soul, both sure and steadfast, and which enters the Presence behind the veil.*" We've touched on this: "the veil" is a Hebraism, which means to enter in through a thinly spread veil, to enter into a door; or in Hebrew culture it meant to enter into the most holy place— referring to the veil in the Jewish temple that separated the inner court from the holy of holies, a very sacred place where God dwelt. That veil, by the way, was thought to be about six inches thick and twenty-two feet tall. However, the veil of the temple was just a shadow of another veil that still exists in the heavenly realms.

When the high priest entered through the veil once a year on the Day of Atonement, they would often tie a rope to his ankle. They would listen for bells on the hem of his robe to determine if he was still alive. If they didn't hear the bells, they could pull him out by the rope around his ankle if need be. Through the finished work of Jesus Christ, we have the liberty and the luxury of entering through the veil, passing behind the veil, passing into the heavenly realms, passing into the glory of God to see and hear what our Father is doing. Because of the blood of Jesus, we no longer have to fear dying when we come into His presence. That's good news!

Entering or going behind the veil is synonymous with entering into the heavenly realms. We no longer need to die to access the heavenly dimensions. Hebrews 6 goes on to tell us why that is: for we have a forerunner that *"has entered for us, even Jesus, having become High Priest forever according to the order of Melchizedek"* (v. 20). So what hope is set before us? The hope of passing through the heavens and entering into the *"Presence behind the veil"* (v. 19). In many translations of the Bible the word *Presence* is capitalized, indicating entering in to the very presence or glory of Jehovah or God. And we can access these kinds of supernatural realms through supernatural doors or gates. Again, this is an aspect of the hidden mysteries of the powers of the age to come.

This is the season that the Lord is accelerating this supernatural process. In the midst of this current shaking, the Lord is activating and releasing this spiritual principle in the Kingdom of God to whosoever will. This speaks of supernatural favor with both God and man. But I also believe it speaks of spiritual authority in the heavenly realms. It speaks of being endued and graced with the power and authority in the spiritual realm. In the heavenly places you can be anointed to have the grace gift or power of God and authority of God over demonic realms (see Ephesians 1:18-23). God anoints you and gives you the ability to discern and to pass through spiritual gates into the Kingdom of Heaven.

Spiritual Authority to Open Up the Heavenly Realms

I believe God is raising up mature sons and daughters of God who have spiritual authority to open up doors in the Godly dimensions and close doors that lead to ungodly dimensions. A good illustration of this point would be the sons of Sceva. In the following passage of scripture, we see that some itinerant Jewish exorcists trying to cast out demons in the name of Jesus because they had seen others do it and they had an encounter with a demonic power. We read about this in Acts 19:13-15:

> *Then some of the itinerant Jewish exorcists took it upon themselves to call the name of the Lord Jesus over those who had evil spirits, saying, "We exorcise you by the Jesus whom Paul preaches." Also there were seven sons of Sceva, a Jewish chief priest, who did so. And the evil spirit answered and said, "Jesus I know, and Paul I know; but who are you?"*

The reason I wanted to look at this is because this scripture illustrates this dynamic: in the spiritual realm, demonic entities recognize those who have legitimate God-given authority (*ischus*, mighty; *kratos*, delegated dominion power; and *exousia*, delegated authority) of the Kingdom of God. And God is raising up mature sons and daughters of God who will walk

67

in the power of Heaven and who will have true God-given and ordained authority in the spiritual realm.

I believe we have stepped into a God-ordained moment of time when the Lord is releasing this kind of supernatural authority to His friends to open up doors, to open up spiritual gates, to open up portals. I have a friend who came upon a portal that opened up and fifty-carat gemstones fell from the heavenly realms. There has been a season where that has happened periodically in certain geographic places. But what if it could happen all of the time to anyone? I believe we have stepped into that day. I believe we have stepped into that hour. I believe there are supernatural gates, supernatural portals or windows, into the spiritual dimensions that God is releasing to you. The Lord will empower you with true God-given and ordained authority to open and close gates in the spiritual dimensions.

Remember, there are Godly spiritual dimensions; but on the other hand, there are also spiritual gates that open up into demonic dimensions. These need to be closed. So what we are talking about is having the authority to bind evil plans and nefarious schemes where they are released through such evil gates of darkness. In the next chapter I want to investigate the believer's authority to open and close spiritual gates. Again, I believe that this is one of the hidden mysteries of the powers of the age to come.

CHAPTER 8

Possessing the Gates of Your Enemies

Let's look at Matthew 16 where Jesus taught about spiritual gates. Again, this illustrates a spiritual principle. Peter had just received an amazing revelation that Jesus Christ was, indeed, the Messiah. In verses 17-18 of Matthew 16 Jesus taught the disciples saying:

> *Blessed are you, Simon Bar-Jonah, for flesh and blood has not revealed this to you, but My Father who is in heaven. And I also say to you that you are Peter, and on this rock I will build My church, and the gates of Hades shall not prevail against it.*

The word translated "prevail" really means to open. What Jesus is really saying is, "Peter, I am giving you and the church authority [*ischus*, mighty; *kratos*, delegated dominion power; and *exousia*, delegated authority] to shut demonic gates or doors. That is an amazing declaration of spiritual truth.

Continuing with verse 19, Jesus says, "*And I will give you the keys of the kingdom of heaven, and whatever you bind on earth*

69

will be bound in heaven, and whatever you loose on earth will be loosed in heaven." What are keys for? Keys open and close doors, do they not? The Greek word translated "gates" in verse 18 can mean gates but is also similar to a plant or a leaf opening and closing.

Spiritual gates open and they close. They don't always open and remain open indefinitely; most spiritual gates open and then they close periodically. This word can also be translated to mean a door that swings both ways. So when God opens a door in the heavenly realms, we can ascend or cross over or penetrate behind the veil and step into the heavenly realms. And, the heavenly realms can also be poured out upon us. Again, this veil between heaven and earth is becoming much more translucent and porous at this hour. This is the double-edged nature of spiritual gates; they open both ways.

I believe that there are many supernatural openings and supernatural gates like this. I don't believe this was something that was relegated to the Old Testament. I don't believe this was something that was relegated to the first-century church. I believe that this is something that has always been part of the Kingdom of God. And I believe there is an acceleration of God releasing to His children, to His friends, spiritual authority to open and close spiritual doors today. I refer to saints like this as apostolic gate keepers.

This places a whole new meaning on the duties of the apostle. The Lord wants His Bride, His church, to wake up and realize and to discern the power and authority that He has given us over spiritual gates. The Lord wants us to understand that we can open and close these types of gates and these types of doors just as Jesus Himself describes in Matthew 16:17-19. Perhaps, you should ponder that passage for a season and invite the Spirit of God to open up the revelation it contains to your spirit more fully.

The Kingdom of Heaven Within You

This is exciting! I believe that it can be life changing for you. Not only can you get the spiritual gates and the heavens opened up over your church and your city and your ministry, but you can get the heavens opened up over your individual life. In fact, God can give His trusted friends spiritual authority to open or close spiritual gates in the heavenly realms. Perhaps God will empower you to open or close a spiritual gate that is associated with a celestial body. In my opinion, this is one of the hidden mysteries of the powers of the age to come. As we have learned in Deuteronomy 28:12, it is God's good pleasure to give us the open heavens. Again, this is an aspect of the hidden mysteries of the powers of the age to come.

The very first blessing that God gave to Abraham, as recorded in Genesis 22:17, came in such a place. This is directly related to what Jesus said in Matthew 16:19: "*I will give you the keys of the kingdom of heaven.*" You see, having the keys to the Kingdom of Heaven is directly related to the gates of hell not prevailing against us. Why? Because the Kingdom of Heaven and its King *are* within you (Luke 17:21)! Sometimes you just need an understanding and true revelation of who you *really* are in Christ. You just need to recognize and believe in the legitimate Kingdom power and authority that God has granted to you through the finished work of Jesus Christ of Nazareth.

We have heard the blessing God speaks over Abraham in Genesis 22 many times, but I want to make sure you get the full revelation. Often a part of a scripture is shared and not the whole concept, so let's look at it in context. In Genesis 22:17 God Almighty is speaking to Abraham saying, *"Blessing I will bless you, and multiplying I will multiply your descendants* [generational blessings] *as the stars of the heaven and as the sand which is on the seashore; and your descendants shall possess the gate of their enemies."* Do you want to do that?

We are often taught about the blessings of Abraham in reference to prosperity, riches, and material wealth; but one of the most significant benefits of having the blessings of Abraham activated in your life is getting the heavens open over your life so you possess the gates of your enemy. Let me submit to you that these are spiritual gates. In fact, the Hebrew word translated "possess" in Genesis 22 means to drive out with authority, to drive out with power, or to dispossess one's foe. Do you want to do that? Also, in Jewish culture the gates were a place of judgment. So when God promises Abraham that he would possess the gates of his enemies, the connotation is that God would give him the power to have judgment over his enemies.

The Season of the Double Doors

Going back to Isaiah 45, we realize there is a lot of hidden revelation in this chapter of Scripture. As I sat in my office in Moravian Falls, the winds of heaven came in and God began to breathe upon this passage of Scripture to release revelation and spiritual truth as you read this book. In Isaiah 45:1 we read, *"To open before him the double doors."* What that really means is two-leaved gates, similar to the gates Jesus referred to in Matthew 16:17-19. This is not a regular way to open a gate. It means to open up wide—specifically to loosen, to plow, to carve, to make appear, to break forth or to break open wide, to draw out, to let go free, to be set free (as in the gates of a prison), to loose or to set free, or to be in an open place or a place of blessing. It means to put off shackles or heavy burdens, to make unstoppable, or to vent or allow light to penetrate into a dark place. Do you want some of that type of Kingdom authority to operate in your life and ministry? It can! This is actually called total salvation (*sozo*).

The shaking will increase, but in the midst of the shaking God is giving his friends supernatural grace to access the gates of heaven. This is the season of the double doors. This is the time of the double portion. This is the season that God is going to allow the Body of Christ to possess the gates of our enemies. So when the Lord goes before us to open the gates or supernatural doors, it has a wonderful compound and supernatural connotation—multiple connotations. It speaks of the Lord God Jehovah opening up the spiritual realm (the open heavens) for you.

I believe with all of my heart as you study this book that there is going to be a grace for impartation for open heavens. Let me encourage you to "believe to receive"! On November 25, 2001, I saw the windows of heaven open and I saw Jesus descend into a small church in Springdale, Newfoundland, Canada. Ever since that time there's been a grace upon my life. The Holy Spirit allows and releases me to freely give that impartation to His people as He wills (Matthew 10:7-8). I believe that same grace is present on this book for you to receive that impartation of open heavens. If you are reading this, you can receive that impartation. Just believe to receive!

Fellowship with Jesus

We must always remember that doors like this can only be discerned when the Lord reveals them or when the Lord releases the grace to you to discern them. Here is an encouraging testimony written in detail in one of my previous books. When I was first saved (born from above), I would go to heaven almost every day for about nine months and I would fellowship with Jesus. My favorite place to go was the great banquet hall. I would just lay there at the feet of Jesus and absorb His glory. The great banquet hall is so beautiful and so big. The Superdome would be tiny compared to the great banquet hall. There are these tables lined up with thousands and thousands of place settings already there; the china, the crystal glasses, everything is ready for the wedding supper of the Lamb. I would go there and I would fellowship with Jesus. I have gone many, many, many times to that place behind the veil between heaven and earth.

One day as I was fellowshipping with the Lord, He said, *"Come with Me. I want to show you something."* I thought, "Great! Maybe we are going to go to Psalm 23; maybe we're going to go to the still waters. Maybe we are going to go to the manicured gardens. Maybe we are going to go to the vineyard." I just love to go to all these different places in heaven with Jesus. (If you would like to discover what your heavenly home looks like read my book *Angels in the Realms of Heaven*.)

But this day the Lord took me down along the rear (western) wall of the great banquet hall. It looks kind of like a castle you might see in medieval times. The walls are made of these stones—beautiful, incredible craftsmanship with no seams between them. I have no idea how they could build it with no mortar or anything; the stones fit perfectly together. The Lord stopped at one point and looked intently at the wall and also instructed me to "look." I looked and said, "Lord, I don't see anything." He said, "*Look again.*" When I looked again the wall began to start to fade in and out like a mirage.

Jesus was teaching me about the seer anointing. Then I saw a door materialize in the stone. The Lord wanted me to share with you that discerning spiritual doors can at times be the same as this. This type of spiritual discernment is an aspect of the seer anointing. The Lord allowed me watch as this door opened. It went up a long pathway to the throne room, and we entered into the throne room that particular evening—an amazing place, the throne room!

God Reveals Spiritual Gates

The point I want to make is that God has to reveal these types of supernatural gates and these types of supernatural doors for you. Sometimes spiritual gates are hidden in plain sight. And when this happens, when God releases you to see and discern these heavenly truths, God releases into your life supernatural blessings. There is supernatural favor that comes with both God and man when you begin to walk in this type of discernment. I call it the seer anointing—when you begin to discern supernatural truths, when you begin to perceive spiritual gates. You begin to pass behind the veil. As we learned, Jesus Christ the royal Priest according to the order of Melchizedek was the Forerunner who blazed this kind of supernatural trail for us. When you follow our Forerunner behind the veil into spiritual realms (Godly dimensions) through spiritual gates like this, there is grace and favor that comes upon you. The fragrance of heaven attaches itself to your person and upon your life. You supernaturally begin to prosper in all aspects of your life.

I believe many of you reading this are in a God-ordained geographical location, a Mahanaim, at a God-ordained (*kairos*) moment of time to receive a blessing from Almighty God. The anointing is like this; it's a double anointing and it's like everything you touch prospers. In the next chapter I will continue to share more keys that can empower you to possess the gates of your enemies and to access and activate the blessings of the heavenly realms into your life through open heavens.

CHAPTER 9

Understanding Spiritual Gates and Open Heavens

Continuing in Isaiah 45:1, we read, "*So that the gates will not be shut.*" Psalm 24 encourages us that we can ascend into the habitation, mountain, or holy place of the Lord (vv. 3-4). Although this book is the third of the Seer Trilogy, it was written as a stand-alone book. If you have not read book two of the trilogy, *Unlocking the Hidden Mysteries of the Seer Anointing II; The Blessings of Psalm 24*, I encourage you to read it to grasp the fullness of the revelation in reference to spiritual gates and the blessing of the Father. From there we can be given the grace and heavenly authority to shake the windows or doors of heaven until they are opened. It's important for us to understand this verse: "*So that the gates will not be shut.*" The Hebrew word translated "gates" here is different than the word translated "two-leaved gates" or "double doors" we looked at earlier in the verse.

The word translated "gates" here means an opening. For example, it could be a door or a gate, specifically the gate to a strong or well guarded city or the gate to a fortified city or a fortified door; but it can also mean a gate or port. Today we might call supernatural gates like these portals. Perhaps you might be thinking that terminology is new age jargon? No, everything the occult operates in is a counterfeit of the real Kingdom—the Kingdom of Heaven. The new age and the occult operate in spiritual truth, laws, and/or principles that were stolen from the Kingdom of God. The issue becomes that the truth is twisted and there is a perversion of God's precious and beautiful spiritual truths (Genesis 3:1). You see, the devil is a liar and the father of lies and deception (John 8:44; 1 John 3:8). So it's not new age, it's scriptural. There are portals like this in the heavenly realms. Some prefer to "Christianize" it and call it open heavens; it makes them feel more comfortable. The Bible refers to openings into the spiritual realms like this as doors, gates, or windows of heaven. Revelation 4:1, John 1:51, Genesis 7:11, Genesis 8:2, 2 Kings 7:19, Malachi 3:10, Luke 3:21, Psalm 78:23, Mark 7:34, Acts 10:11, and Revelation 19:11 are just a few references to this scriptural dynamic.

The thing I want you to see is that gates like this are continually open over some people's lives. Do you know some people that prosper no matter what happens? Abraham, after Melchizedek spoke a blessing over him, lived under an open heaven. Everything that he touched prospered. Some people are like that; if you give them lemons they make lemonade—it doesn't matter what happens in their life, they prosper from it. That's because they have this type of spiritual dynamic operating in their lives; they are living under an open heaven. The grace of God rests upon them.

How do we get the heavens opened up over our lives to release the Lord's grace and favor upon us? One example would be found in Matthew 17 where Peter, James, and John were taken by Jesus to a specific geographical place (the Mount of Transfiguration) at a specific chronological time and they saw Christ transfigured before them. In Acts 4:20 when Peter and John were confronted by the Sanhedrin, who could well have crucified them, they said, "*We cannot but speak the things which we have seen and heard.*"

I believe Peter and John were referring to the Mount of Transfiguration. They were activated into the Godly dimensions during the Mount of Transfiguration experience and entered into Godly discernment and the seer anointing by their proximity to Jesus as He was transfigured. There was a supernatural exchange and impartation that took place at the Mount of Transfiguration. The Lord is still releasing these kinds of transformational experiences today, and through them God is still releasing impartation and activation of the heavenly realities into people's lives.

When God opens up the realms of heaven over your life and you step into this dynamic of the heavenly realms, when heaven becomes real to you and you experience it, it can never be taken from you. I believe you are going to experience a release of God's blessings as you read this book. God's favor, God's power can be poured out upon your life like a river. It can rain down continually to give you fruit in season and out of season. You can be like those trees planted by the river of God in Revelation 22:2: "*In the middle of its street, and on either side of the river, was the tree of life, which bore twelve fruits, each tree yielding its fruit every month. The leaves of the tree were for the healing of the nations."* The leaves of these heavenly trees are always blooming, always bearing fruit, always touching and impacting the nations with healing. You can be transformed into a green olive tree planted in the house of God.

We see this type of Kingdom fruitfulness in Psalm 52:8-9: *"But I am like a green olive tree in the house of God; I trust in the mercy of God forever and ever. I will praise You forever, Because You have done it; And in the presence of Your saints I will wait on Your name, for it is good."* In the midst of evil and shaking, you prosper supernaturally and praise the Lord. Don't listen to the prophets of doom! Put your faith and confidence in the Prophet of Life, Jesus Christ!

Also important to know is that when we possess the gates of our enemies, we can stop them up, we can shut them; we can take the keys of the Kingdom of Heaven and lock the wicked gates or portals that open into the demonic realms. That eliminates the evil and nefarious plans of the enemy from operating in your life and within your sphere of influence.

God Opens Up His Heavens to Rain Down Supernatural Blessings

Places like this are call Mahanaims. In Genesis 32 we read of Jacob, who came to such a place. Jacob's spiritual DNA was to live under an open heaven because of his genealogical line. Your spiritual DNA is also to live under an open heaven. If you are really a born-again believer in this Man named Jesus, the Messiah, the Anointed One, you have been grafted into the tree of life (Romans 11:16-24; Revelation 22:14). You have the same spiritual DNA as Jesus Christ of Nazareth; and therefore, you have the right to live your life under an open heaven like we see here in Genesis 32. You can learn to pass behind the veil to receive heavenly blessings. You can learn to enter into the presence and glory of God to activate a transformation in your life. You can learn to possess the spiritual gates of your enemy.

Beginning with verses 1 and 2, we read, "*So Jacob went on his way, and the angels of God met him. When Jacob saw them...*" What happens? The seer anointing activates in his life. He came to a place where the heavens were opened; and in that place of open heavens, his spiritual senses were activated so that he could see and hear from the heavenly realms. Jacob discerned a spiritual gate or portal that opened into Godly dimensions or into what Christians call heaven. Jacob discerned and saw the activity of heaven in the earthly or temporal dimension.

In Luke 3:21-22 we read where Jesus came to John to be baptized. We see in verse 21 an amazing supernatural occurrence: "*It came to pass that Jesus also was baptized; and while He prayed, the heaven was opened.*" The scripture in verse 22 says that while He was being baptized those present in that geographical place saw the Holy Spirit descend bodily in the form of a dove—"*And the Holy Spirit descended in bodily form like a dove upon Him*"—and they heard the voice of the Father saying, "*You are My beloved Son; in You I am well pleased.*" What was that? That was an example of a Mahanaim. That was an example of the heavens opening up. That was an example of Deuteronomy 28:12. God opened up His good treasure the heavens and rained blessings down upon people. The people discerned and saw the activity of heaven in the earthly or temporal dimension.

When Jesus prayed that day at the River Jordan and the heavens opened and the Holy Spirit descended and God the Father spoke in an audible voice, they never closed—the heavens never closed. The Creator sent His Son, Jesus Christ of Nazareth, on a mission of mercy to the earth to open up the heavens over mankind. The Creator reopened the heavens over mankind so the creature could have communion with the Creator. Again, this dynamic is one of the hidden mysteries of the powers of the age to come. Jesus was walking in the understanding that He could see what His Father was doing by discerning spiritual gates or open heavens. And the Lord has encouraged us to do greater things than He Himself accomplished (John 14:12).

Human Mahanaims

I believe that God is raising up mature sons and mature daughters who will pray with the authority to open the heavens over their heads. When this happens they will ascend into the heavenly dimensions and see what the Father is doing and hear what the Father is saying. As they decree and model those same things with their actions, they will manifest the Kingdom of Heaven upon earth like we see demonstrated in Luke 3. These mature sons and mature daughters will walk under open heavens like Christ and will be human Mahanaims or open heavens everywhere they go. Again, this is one of the hidden mysteries of the powers of the age to come. God will give His friends unusual levels of spiritual authority to open the heavens into the Godly dimensions. On the other hand, I believe, the Father will also give these arising mature sons and daughters a similar spiritual authority to bind or close gates into demonic dimensions. Again, I call these kinds of mature sons and daughters of the Most High God apostolic gate keepers.

We see in Genesis 32:2, when Jacob saw the angels, that "*he said, 'This is God's camp.' And he called the name of that place Mahanaim*." *Mahanaim* is another Hebrew word that can mean double camp or double doors, as we see in Isaiah 45. In the Hebrew culture a Mahanaim was a place of blessing and a place of communing with Almighty God, Jehovah—the same One who wants to hold your right hand.

A Mahanaim is a place of open heavens, a place where the blessings of Jehovah are released from the heavenly realms into the earthly realms. This is a place of blessing. A Mahanaim is a gate or portal that opens into the heavenly dimensions. There were times when Jesus operated in this dynamic and released the Kingdom of Heaven upon earth in His sphere of influence by discerning and working within open heavens, or a Mahanaim, and with power and authority of the Father (John 1:51). At times this can involve recognizing and co-laboring with God's angels. In other instances it can be that we learn to discern the different types of glory that is pouring out into our sphere in influence through Godly spiritual gates. Then we just decree and prophesy into that particular manifestation of the glory of God.

We can easily work creative miracles when we discern that a spiritual gate of heaven is open and that the glory of God for creative miracles—for example, being released by the Lord and is in fact present. Then we learn to co-labor with the Holy Spirit and the angels of the Lord. We decree and we create supernatural manifestations of the Kingdom of God with our God-inspired words. This is a similar pattern to the one in which that Jesus operated and worked miracles. We see a scriptural example of this supernatural pattern in Romans 4:17: "*In the presence* [glory of God] *of Him whom he believed— God who gives life to the dead and calls those things which do not exist as though they did.*

When the creative glory of God manifests in our meetings as we discern a spiritual gate or open heaven (God releases or pours out His glory in our presence), then we can simply decree or speak into the hovering of the creative glory of God (Elohim) and creative miracles happen. These can include new teeth forming or gold crowns, gold fillings, or even new enamel forming on teeth. I call those kinds of creative miracles dental miracles. However, God is not limited.

We have seen creative miracles where people have had damaged or missing glands or major internal organs created, fingers and/or toes grow back, or metal dissolve out of bodies—to name a few of the miracles God is releasing in the earth at this hour. In fact, my wife, Kathy, accidentally cut off about three eighths of an inch of her right index finger in Jerusalem in 2011. As we operated in and rested in the glory in this manner, her finger grew back 100 percent, including the missing fingernail.

By the way, Kathy also has supernaturally received two golden crowns in our meetings as well as nine new teeth (new enamel reformed and replaced amalgam and damaged teeth)! I believe that these kinds of miracles are an aspect of the power of the Father combined with the power and anointing of the Holy Spirit. This is true unity of the Spirit. I will outline this in more detail in a later chapter. But I want to mention to you that this kind of power is different than the anointing of the Holy Spirit alone, although the anointing of the Holy Spirit certainly factors into these kinds of creative miracles. Think about that.

This is a practical aspect of one of the supernatural hidden mysteries of the powers of the age to come. You can co-labor with God in the glory realms to release amazing miracles, signs, and wonders. Another sign and wonder that we are seeing on a frequent and regular basis in our meetings is the Lord releasing the fragrances of heaven into our gatherings. This has happened dozens of times in several nations. The wonderful smell of roses or cinnamon or other heavenly aromas just begin to be poured out in the meetings. People even discern these heavenly fragrances over the internet in other nations! There are no limitations in the glory or in the spiritual dimensions.

This sign and wonder truly blesses those in attendance and forces those who may have some doubt or questions about the Kingdom of Heaven to seriously "wonder" about the reality of Jesus the Messiah. All of these things are for the glory of God! All of these things are heavenly blessings that come into geographic places where there are spiritual gates or open heavens unfolding. The good news is that you can get the heavens open over your life and live this kind of supernatural lifestyle.

A Supernatural Exchange Between Heaven and Earth

In places where the gates of heaven are open, there is a transfer of heavenly treasures or blessings into the earthly realm and into the lives of the people or God's friends who are present. At times individuals can carry this aspect of open heavens everywhere they go! This is real; it's a true dynamic in the Kingdom of Heaven. It's an ongoing dynamic today, too. There can be a supernatural exchange between the heavenly realms and the earthly realms. When gates like this are opened, God still pours out His blessings today. Isn't this exciting! Again, this is another of the hidden mysteries of the powers of the age to come.

I believe that, if you want it, the Lord can allow you to experience a literal Mahanaim. I believe there will be gates of breakthrough that will manifest and that you will be empowered to pass through and as you go there will be a supernatural blessing released from God Almighty into your life. I believe you can be delivered. I believe you can be healed. I believe you can be set free. I believe you can have your life transformed. I will share several testimonies along this line later in this book. I believe you can be empowered to step into the fullness of your God-ordained destiny. I believe there is a double door of destiny that will manifest in your life as you read this book. God confirms the Gospel: "*The Lord working with them and confirming the word through the accompanying signs*" (Mark 16:20).

In the next chapter I want to touch on a few important scriptural principles that can help to keep you rooted and firmly grounded in the word of God and give you scriptural understanding to help protect you as you begin to prayerfully access these kinds of supernatural gates and spiritual dimensions. Therefore, before I move forward I want to emphasize: there are doors or gates that lead into Godly dimensions; but, on the other hand, there are also gates or doors that lead into demonic or nefarious realms. I believe that we are at a day and an hour when the Lord of Hosts is releasing supernatural revelation and discernment to His people to know the difference between the two (good and evil) as the return of the Lord draws near (Isaiah 5:20). Again, these are, in my opinion, some of the hidden mysteries of the powers of the age to come.

CHAPTER 10

Allowing God to Destroy Demonic Strongholds

Again, I wish to elaborate more fully on the concepts from *Unlocking the Hidden Mysteries of the Seer Anointing II: The Blessings of Psalm 24* in this part of this book. Let's continue to look at the revelation found in Isaiah 45. I want to unlock some of these hidden mysteries concerning spiritual gates and supernatural doors. We need to understand this dynamic of the spiritual realms. Many people who lack mature discernment can become trapped or caught up into ungodly dimensions without being aware of exactly where they are. This is never a good thing; and it is the result of being undiscerning, which in my opinion is a sin (Romans 1:31). In my opinion, the lack of Godly spiritual discernment is possible one of the greatest sins or strongholds in the Body of Christ at this hour.

In the area where I currently abide there is a lot of supernatural activity because there is a series of spiritual gates in the mountains. Not all of the spiritual gates in Moravian Falls, North Carolina, open into Godly dimensions. Sedona, Arizona, is another example of a geographical place where there are numerous gates or doors that open into the spiritual dimensions. In fact, in Sedona you can pay spiritual guides to take you on a "vortex tour." These spiritual guides will take you to the main three vortexes or portals in the area.

Moravian Falls also has a "nickel tour" of the "hotspots," but some of these are not always open to the public. I want to reaffirm that not all spiritual gates are good or healthy to access, and that is why you need to be mature and have Godly discernment in this area. You need to develop your seer anointing and gifting. You need to have wisdom and be led by the Holy Spirit rather than spiritual guides. Be careful of counterfeit (ungodly) supernatural activity. If the Holy Spirit has not given you the spiritual authority to access spiritual gates, it can be a dangerous practice. People who trespass unaware into spiritual gates often become sick, infirmed, oppressed, and at times spiritually bankrupt. This is a serious business and I pray that you will heed this warning. Tread carefully in these kind of supernatural adventures. Again, not all spiritual gates are healthy or wise to access.

The prophet Isaiah made this amazing statement about discernment or rather the lack there of. "*Woe to those who call evil good, and good evil; Who put darkness for light, and light for darkness; Who put bitter for sweet, and sweet for bitter!*" (Isaiah 5:20). In my opinion, one of the greatest areas of need in the Body of Christ is Godly discernment. If you have read the first book in this Seer Trilogy, you will know that we can learn to discern with our spiritual senses by reason of use according to the spiritual principle of Hebrews 5:14.

Unfortunately, today may of us have our spiritual eyes blinded by the god of this world and our spiritual ears are dull (hard of hearing spiritually). The prophet Isaiah also spoke of this sinful condition in Isaiah 6:9-10; *"Go, and tell this people: 'Keep on hearing, but do not understand; Keep on seeing, but do not perceive.' Make the heart of this people dull, And their ears heavy, And shut their eyes; Lest they see with their eyes, And hear with their ears, And understand with their heart, And return and be healed."* God wants for His children to both see and hear what He is doing so that we can co-labor with Him.

The Creator of the heavens and the earth wants for you to have ears that will hear and eyes that will see well (into the spiritual realm where God dwells). The Lord wants for us to be restored, to return to Him, and to be healed or made whole and complete. I love what my new friend Dr. James Maloney teaches in his wonderful book *The Dancing Hand of God*. We must learn to discern the difference in the Holy and the profane. We must become mature sons and daughters of God who can discern the difference between good and evil. I highly recommend that you read *The Dancing Hand of God*.

Slimed

Many times people (Christians and non-believers) come to certain geographic places seeking supernatural encounters and are successful in tapping into the spiritual dimensions. Be reminded that not all supernatural experiences are from God. Sometimes they tap into ungodly spirits (demons) and demonic realms without knowing it. Why? The reason is possibly because they have poor or immature discernment.

They become deceived. They tap into ungodly dimensions and demonic powers. Certainly there are deceptive supernatural encounters happening all of the time upon the earth. We need to have the God-given wisdom and discernment in order to differentiate between the two. This dynamic is also true for Jerusalem, which has the most active open heaven upon the earth. However, there is still a lot of counterfeit supernatural activity in Israel today, just as in the past.

As a result of this dynamic, many well-meaning people become defiled by demonic powers because they cannot discern the difference between good and evil. Consequently, many find themselves corrupted and debased in spirit, soul, and body by accessing the ungodly spiritual dimensions. To state that in Christianeze (yes, that is a new word), these undiscerning people get hung up in the second heaven or ungodly spiritual dimensions and get "slimed." *Slimed* is another Christianeze term that means spiritually defiled. Danger, Will Robinson! Again, it bears repeating; People who trespass unaware into ungodly spiritual gates often become sick, infirmed, oppressed, and at times spiritually bankrupt. This is a serious business, and I pray that you will heed this warning. Tread carefully in this kind of supernatural adventures. Again, not all spiritual gates are healthy or wise to access.

In the second heaven there are evil and demonic forces that move around in that area of the heavenly dimensions. Therefore, you need to rise above the swirl and stink of the second heaven and access the literal, real realms of heaven. You need to pass through the second heaven to come up higher. So, it is very important that you develop your spiritual discernment to know when you are tapping into unholy things. This is the principle found in Hebrews 5:14: *"Solid food belongs to those who are of full age, that is, those who by reason of use have their senses exercised to discern both good and evil."*

The Fullness of His Destiny in You

We are speaking of becoming mature in our spiritual discernment. We are speaking of becoming mature sons and daughters of the Most High God. Many people have zeal but have little or no wisdom. We need both. We need the power of the Spirit that is grounded in the Truth of the word of God, the Scripture. This is another message, and I want to move back to the point at hand. I believe that this is an unfolding dynamic at this hour and that anyone can tap into or access these types of heavenly blessings from the Kingdom of God, but we must certainly do so with wisdom. I recommend that you read my book *Dancing with Angels #1* and the first two books of the Seer Trilogy, *Unlocking the Hidden Mysteries of the Seer Anointing I* and *II*. These books can give you more in-depth understanding on this important subject that can help to both empower and protect you.

Demonic Yokes of Darkness

Returning to Isaiah 45 we see that God goes before us to break open doors and to shatter any locks or hindrances that keep us from walking in the fullness of His destiny for us. We see in verse 2 that God says, *"I will go before you And make the crooked places straight."* This speaks of a transfer of wealth. The Lord will give you the honor (glory) and the riches of your enemy. It gets better: "*I will break in pieces the gates of bronze.*" This speaks of shattering the strongholds of the enemy, destroying demonic oppression, destroying sickness, and releasing you from a spirit of poverty and depression or any other oppression the enemy has placed upon you in your spirit, soul, and body through demonic yokes of darkness. These strongholds of the enemy—sickness, poverty, depression, and oppression—often activate in a person's life through open doors of darkness that open into the ungodly dimensions. That is why you need to close doors in your life that are open into ungodly dimensions. Sometimes closing these doors that open into the demonic dimensions can release a miraculous transformation and healing in your life and even in your entire family.

Going back to Isaiah 45:2, the prophet goes on: "*And cut the bars of iron.*" What this language means is to utterly destroy the head of the gate, ruler of the gate, or to utterly destroy the king of the gates of darkness. Remember verse 1 where it says God holds our hands so He will loose the armor or the loins of kings. It is possibly speaking of demonic powers. This speaks of God giving us victory in the spiritual realm that will affect our life and prosperity in the terrestrial, natural, or earthly realm.

We see this outlined again as we go forward in Isaiah 45:3; the Lord says, "*I will give you the treasures of darkness And hidden riches of secret places.*" (This Scripture has a pair of meanings, compound meanings.) "*That you may know that I, the LORD, Who call you by your name, Am the God of Israel.*" So God gives us revelation of His identity by doing these two things.

When the scripture tells us the Lord, Jehovah, will give us, the Hebrew word translated "give" here is not the regular word for give. It has a profound meaning. It means to give liberally or spectacularly or extravagantly, to put someone in a place of power, to make someone, to refashion a thing, to add to, to appoint, to ascribe, to assign, to avenge or to behead your enemies, to bestow, to bring forth, to charge with favor or to give one prominence or glory, to lift up, to ordain, to pay, to recompense, to render, to restore those things that have been sold or stolen, to send out, to set forth, to send upon a mission, to show secret treasures, to shoot forth or shoot upward or thrust higher, to yield to God, or to yield to the hand of God.

Remember, in verse 1 we saw how we can be helped by the hand of God when we learn to submit to the Lord and allow the Lord to hold our hand. This posture is not a posture of meekness; but this type of submission is a posture of spiritual maturity, becoming mature sons and daughters of God. Mature sons and daughters of God rest and trust in the Lord.

Two Types of Treasures

We see two types of treasures God wants to give to us as these gates are destroyed and/or opened before us as the Holy Spirit wills; the key to unlocking these Kingdom blessings in your life is to be in submission to Him. The first type of treasures comes from the heavenly dimensions and these are blessings that God has preordained for you to have and enjoy. These can be grace, favor, anointing, revelation, the abiding power of His presence upon you, and many more heavenly blessings. These are the hidden riches of secret places (heavenly realms).

The second type of treasures that the Lord wished to restore to you is treasures of darkness that the evil one has stolen from you. These are hidden treasures of darkness that are hidden in the demonic spiritual realms or dimensions. Ephesians 6:12 describes this dynamic and the demonic forces which control such treasure of darkness: *"For we do not wrestle against flesh and blood, but against principalities, against powers, against the rulers of the darkness of this age, against spiritual hosts of wickedness in the heavenly places."* Again, some theologians call this area of the spiritual dimensions the second heaven. In reality, I believe that the universe consists of innumerable dimensions or levels of heaven and other spiritual places. Not all of the spiritual dimensions are good. (See Deuteronomy 10:14; 1 Kings 8:27; 2 Chronicles 2:6, Nehemiah 9:6.)

Ungodly Spiritual Dimensions

So hell, for example, is a type of spiritual dimension that most people would not welcome or consider a good place. Here is a short sermon for you: Heaven good. Hell bad, don't go there. Again, hell would be an example of ungodly spiritual dimension.

You may have a genealogical blessing in your generation line that has been blocked or stolen by the evil one from your great-great-grandfather. The Lord can restore that blessing. It could be, for example, a supernatural gift for prospering in business or science. The enemy has dark places in the ungodly dimensions where he has storehouses of stolen treasures. These demonic strongholds or storehouses are guarded by rulers of darkness and other demonic forces. They are seques-tered away in vaults of darkness that are guarded by demonic powers in the ungodly spiritual realms. There is a key to unlocking this hidden mystery in Isaiah 45. These genealogical blessings can be hidden behind demonic spiritual gates or doors.

The first is when Isaiah 45 says in verse 3: "*I will give you the treasures of darkness.*" The word translated "treasures" means a depository, an armory, a guarded cellar, a storehouse, or secret treasure or treasure house, just like we saw in verse 2. Today we refer to places like this as Fort Knox. Jesus said in John 10:10, "*The thief does not come except to steal, and to kill, and to destroy. I have come that they may have life, and that they may have it more abundantly.*" Where do you think the enemy keeps all those things he has stolen from humanity over the millennia?

They are in storehouses of darkness. God wants to burst open the double doors of the storehouses of darkness and restore to His people the treasures, the anointings, the gifts of God, the material wealth that has been stolen from His people. These treasures could be gifts and callings that were given by God but which were corrupted by the enemy. These corrupted treasures can be restored and utilized for God's glory. However, the treasures of darkness can also mean misery, destruction, death, ignorance, sorrow, wickedness. Those adjectives describe the results of having God's blessings stolen from someone. Most of the time this is allowed by individuals unwittingly; and many times these are generational curses that individuals had no role in activating. However, they are still subject to these evil and nefarious demonic devices of misery, death, ignorance, sorrow, poverty, despair, sadness, unfruitfulness, and so on.

Everything the enemy has taken, every evil plan and yoke of darkness that the enemy has placed upon us, God wants to turn around according to Romans 8:28: *"All things work together for good to those who love God, to those who are the called according to His purpose."* God's heart and plans for us are good and His desire for us is to prosper and to be in health (3 John 1:2). The Father desires to restore to us every good thing that has been stolen from us and from our spiritual destiny through our previous generational descendants. When the Lord allows us to possess the gates of our enemies, He can at times give us the hidden treasures of darkness. When this happens the Lord supernaturally reverses the curses upon our lives and we are supernaturally healed of sickness in our bodies, delivered of demonic oppression, and set free to prosper and be in health!

God can turn generational curses into generational blessings when we get the revelation and appropriate the keys to access these kinds of treasures of darkness. The Lord can restore and turn demonic plans around 100 percent to give to us hundredfold blessings in place of the demonic curses that may be opposing God's best for our lives. This is a supernatural exchange that God initiates in the glory realms as we learn to rest in Him. Of course the key to this process is accepting Jesus Christ as your Lord and Savior. If you would like to make sure that you are saved or "born from above" (what the church calls "born again"), just turn to the prayers in the back of this book and pray the prayer of salvation now.

That has literally happened in my life. I lost a lot of things; I lost lands, I lost homes, I lost money, I lost businesses. Everything I lost God has restored to me at least a hundredfold. I began to walk this out unknowingly by stepping behind the veil, passing through spiritual gates to enter into the presence and glory of God. I simply accessed and rested in God's presence (glory); and when I came back into the earthly realms God's favor, God's grace was just attached to me and everything that I touched prospered. I give God glory for that.

God can literally give back to you the treasures of darkness lost to the enemy in this way. One aspect is taking your God-given spiritual authority and closing gates and doors in your life that lead or open into ungodly dimensions. Learn to enforce your spiritual boundaries and the spiritual gates in your sphere of influence. At times you need to discern and shut such gates for yourself and your family line. This is an aspect of the hidden mysteries of the powers of the age to come. Currently there is an acceleration of this supernatural dynamic of restoration as the Creator of heaven and earth is moving with sovereignty and power in His friend's lives to bring healing and freedom. In the next chapter I will help you understand how to unlock several heavenly blessings which God has stored and kept back for you in the heavenly realms.

CHAPTER 11

Accessing the Spiritual Blessings of the Heavenly Places

The second thing illustrated in Isaiah 45:3 is the *"hidden riches of secret places."* These are heavenly treasures sequestered in the heavenly realms. We see this kind of spiritual blessing or treasure outlined in Ephesians 1:3: *"Blessed be the God and Father of our Lord Jesus Christ, who has blessed us with every spiritual blessing in the heavenly places in Christ."* I personally like this one. There are treasures and blessings the Father has stored up for you in the heavenly dimensions. The hidden riches of secret places can be translated as a secret storehouse—hence a secreted, valuable, buried treasure or treasure house.

Generally it refers to money or wealth; but it can also mean hidden riches such as silver, gold, and valuable herbs and oils—frankincense and myrrh, for example. It can be hidden treasures or treasures that are not fought for or that one does not labor for to own, possess, or create. These are wonderful, Godly blessings associated with learning and discerning to see and open spiritual doors into the heavenly realms. The hidden riches of the secret place are Godly treasures and blessings directly from the heavenly realms. I shared the testimony earlier about how Paul Cox and I accessed hidden treasures of the secret places like this.

The Secret Place of the Most High

As good as these heavenly riches are, it gets even better. The secret place mentioned in Isaiah 45:3 means concealed riches or treasure, not necessarily money or gold or frankincense or myrrh but spiritual riches—treasure hidden in the heavenly realms or the secret place of the Most High. This is treasure hidden in a concealed place or realm or in a secret place. Let's go to Colossians 3:1-2: "*If then you were raised with Christ, seek those things which are above, where Christ is, sitting at the right hand of God. Set your mind on things above, not on things on the earth.*"

Let's look at it again in Ephesians 1:17-19: "*That the God of our Lord Jesus Christ, the Father of glory, may give to you the spirit of wisdom and revelation in the knowledge of Him.*" These are some of the secret and hidden treasures in the heavenly places. Continuing with verse 18: "*The eyes of your understanding being enlightened*" speaks of the seer anointing. And in verses 18-19: "*That you may know what is the hope of His calling, what are the riches of the glory of His inheritance in the saints, and what is the exceeding greatness of His **power** toward us who believe, according to the working of His mighty **power***" (emphasis added). This speaks of *dunamis* (miracle working power) and *kratos* (delegated dominion power and authority).

God is giving to His people that *kratos* power to open up doors to the heavenly realms. By the way, accessing the heavenly dimensions is a type of spiritual blessing. That's your inheritance. Verse 20 tells us about that *dunamis* power "which He worked in Christ when He raised Him from the dead and seated Him at His right hand in the heavenly places." That's your inheritance too. We can be seated with Christ in heavenly places. We can pass behind the veil. We can come into the very presence of God. Then we can discern the prayers of Christ, rest in Him, and allow Him to work on our behalf; thus releasing *dunamis,* miracle working power, and *kratos*, delegated dominion power, in our spheres of influence in the terrestrial or earthly realm.

When this happens, we begin to live our lives in the glory realm. Verse 21 tells us where the heavenly places are located: *"Far above all principality and power and might and dominion, and every name that is named, not only in this age but also in that which is to come."* When we begin to discern and learn how to open up spiritual gates to pass through them to rest in the glory of God, we can enter into the heavenly dimensions and rise above this earth and the shakings that are filling the world with fear and great trepidation.

This is why Isaiah 26:3 is such an important prophetic promise for the Body of Christ: *"You will keep him in perfect peace, Whose mind is stayed on You, Because he trusts in You."* Paul also tells us to *"set your mind on things above"* (Colossians 3:2). When we can keep our minds, our spirits, our souls, and our bodies focused on Christ and His Kingdom, we rise above the cares of this present age and we begin to live a lifestyle of glory. No matter what's happening around us, we are just walking in the FOG—the favor of God. We are in the glory, and in the glory Christ's Kingdom just manifests everywhere we go.

Dwelling in the Secret Place

Really what we are talking about is living our life according to Psalm 91. This is important. The hidden riches of the secret places that we are speaking about from Isaiah 45 put a whole new meaning on Psalm 91. Let's read verses 1 and 2: *"He who dwells in the secret place of the Most High Shall abide under the shadow of the Almighty. I will say of the LORD, "He is my refuge and my fortress."* You see, when we abide in the secret place under the wings of Almighty God, He becomes our fortress. Do you know how many powers or principalities are able to break through the doors into the fortress of God? The answer to that is zero, none! And when we purpose in our hearts to make the secret place of the Most High our dwelling place, we are protected by God.

Going on with Psalm 91, we read the end of verse 2 through verse 7:

> *My God, in Him I will trust. Surely He shall deliver you from the snare of the fowler And from the perilous pestilence. He shall cover you with His feathers, And under His wings you shall take refuge; His truth shall be your shield and buckler. You shall not be afraid of the terror by night, Nor of the arrow that flies by day, Nor of the pestilence that walks in darkness, Nor of the destruction that lays waste at noonday. A thousand may fall at your side, And*

ten thousand at your right hand; But it shall not come near you.

Remember, Jesus gave us the keys to the Kingdom of Heaven. The key to living a Psalm 91 lifestyle is that we must purpose in our hearts to make the secret place of the Most High our dwelling place. There is a grace and anointing that is associated with Isaiah 45 in this wonderful Psalm.

So let's return to Isaiah 45 and dig out a few more keys beginning with verse 4: *"For Jacob My servant's sake."* Remember, Jacob received the blessings of God at the Mahanaim that we read about in Genesis 32. Continuing with Isaiah 45:4, we read, *"And Israel My elect, I have even called you by your name; I have named you, though you have not known Me."* This is another Hebraism. The Hebrew word translated "known" here is *yada*; which means to know; or to see; or to experience in a tangible way—to feel, taste, smell, or touch. *Yada* means to discover a friend, to discover kinfolk or a kinsman redeemer, to be allowed to know, to be given knowledge, or to have revelation of God or Jehovah.

The NIV version of this passage of Scripture says, *"I summon you by name and bestow on you a title of honor, though you do not acknowledge me."* We could just say that it is to have the understanding that we can become the friend of God; that we can pass behind the veil and come into the glory to experience the realms of heaven, the glory of God. You see, no longer is heaven "way up there." Heaven is all around us. There is an acceleration of grace and supernatural outpourings at this season. There is a grace being given by God to His friends to know

Him. There is a new release of this kind of grace to access or go behind the veil and enter into the presence and glory of God to know Him more intimately. You can entertain heaven!

There is a wonderful passage of Scripture that I like to remember when I come into the very presence of God. It is in Isaiah 43:26. The Lord speaking, says, "*Put Me in remembrance; Let us contend together; State your case, that you may be acquitted.*" That is what we can learn to experience. We can enter into the presence of God, and we can state our case and remind God that He is a God of mercy; He is a God of grace.

Back to Isaiah 45:5 we read: "*I am the LORD, and there is no other; There is no God besides Me. I will gird you.*" That means He will strengthen you, empower you, and give you everything you need to fulfill your destiny. Continuing with verses 5 through 8, He says:

> *Though you have not known Me. That they may know from the rising of the sun to its setting That there is none besides Me. I am the LORD, and there is no other; I form the light and create darkness, I make peace and create calamity; I, the LORD, do all these things. Rain down, you heavens, from above, And let the skies pour down righteousness; Let the earth open, let them bring forth salvation, And let righteousness spring up together. I, the LORD, have created it.*"

The Book of Proverbs 25:2 says, "*It is the glory of God to conceal a matter, But the glory of kings is to search out a matter.*" You see, God has secrets in the hidden places—secrets, secret treasures, hidden mysteries in the Kingdom of God. There are treasury vaults in the glory realms of heaven that you can access. Revelation 1:5-6 says the blood of Jesus makes us kings and priests. Therefore, you have the liberty to dig these heavenly treasures out. God can protect and empower you to discern and access the hidden treasures of darkness. The Lord can also empower you to access the hidden treasures of the secret places in the heavenly dimensions when we learn to discern spiritual gates.

We find an important scriptural reference to this dynamic in Matthew 2:11, speaking of the Magi, the three kings: *"And when they had come into the house, they saw the young Child with Mary His mother, and fell down and worshiped Him. And when they had opened their treasures, they presented gifts to Him: gold, frankincense, and myrrh."* The King wants to open up the treasures of heaven and present to you gold, frankincense, and myrrh. Gold speaks of material wealth. Frankincense speaks of the presence of God, the glory of God. Myrrh speaks of healing, miracles, signs, and wonders. In the next chapter I will share a powerful testimony of what it might look like when the powers of the age to come manifest to release the power of the Kingdom with miracles, signs, and wonders in your sphere of influence.

CHAPTER 12

Accessing the Hidden Treasures and Mysteries of the Kingdom

I believe that the Lord is opening up these kinds of hidden treasures and revealing these secret mysteries of the Kingdom of God at this hour. An extraordinary manifestation of the Kingdom occurred one Sunday evening at the School of the Seers #5 and we were given revelation that God would begin to release other dimensions. We understood that spiritual doors would be opened to experience "Godly dimensions" for those in attendance of the final meeting much like we learned about in Isaiah 45 and Psalm 91.

In addition to this we believed that the Lord would release to His people the authority to close spiritual gates that led into ungodly dimensions in their sphere of influence. These ungodly doors also allowed evil and nefarious spirits to enter into the lives of people and also into geographic areas such as cities, counties, states, and even nations. I believe that we actually experienced corporate deliverance as generational curses lifted off of the land surrounding the Moravian Falls, North Carolina, region.

I believe that God is training and raising up supernatural gate keepers at this hour! These apostolic gate keepers will minister in this level of Kingdom authority and power.

We also understood that many who would step into and through those doors into Godly dimensions would be healed, set free, and empowered as ungodly doors and spiritual gates would be closed and Godly doors would be opened in their lives. In fact, all of those things transpired on the final meeting; and it seemed that heaven truly invaded earth and an amazing manifestation of the Kingdom occurred at the School of the Seers on Sunday, May 4, 2013, at the 7 p.m. meeting.

During the meeting as Paul Cox and I ministered and shared the Gospel of the Kingdom in unity and love, the realms of heaven began to invade earth. (Unity and love are important keys to releasing these kinds of hidden and mysterious treasures of the Kingdom of Heaven. It may not be possible to touch this level of the Kingdom power without unity and the God kind of love.) At one point there was no longer any need to preach as doors were opened into the heavenly dimensions (Revelation 4:1). Through the giftings and anointings of the leadership of the meeting, we discerned that a door was indeed opened into the heavenly realms. In addition to this we "saw" and understood that members of the great cloud of witnesses were entering into the meeting through these spiritual doors, gates, or portals that had opened from the heavenly dimensions into the School of the Seers (Hebrews 12:1).

At first we discerned that one from the great cloud of witnesses had stepped out of heaven and stepped into the meeting. It was interesting to note that as this occurred, the power and glory of God filled the room. We soon discovered that the power and glory of God was most powerful and tangible at the spot that we discerned this Godly spiritual being to be standing. I walked over to actually feel with my right hand the things that I was discerning in the spiritual realm. Is it possible that the great cloud of witnesses might not be made perfect apart from us? Perhaps that connection will happen on the earthly or temporal realm and not after the rapture in heaven? The Book of Hebrews tells us about members of our heavenly family or the great cloud of witnesses: *"And all these, having obtained a good testimony through faith, did not receive the promise, God having provided something better for us, that they should not be made perfect apart from us"* (Hebrews 11:39-40).

This is in my opinion another aspect of the powers of the age to come. As we have learned the veil between heaven and earth has become and is becoming thinner and more translucent than ever before. As a result, when these invasions of the heavenly realms come, there may be times when members of the great cloud of witnesses will step into our meetings and into our sphere of influence. In some supernatural way this will complete their earthy journey.

In my opinion, one scriptural example of this dynamic of the powers of the age to come is the appearance of Moses at the Mount of Transfiguration. We know that Moses certainly died and was buried (Deuteronomy 34:7). However, we must also remember that our God is not the God of the dead but the God of the living. Jesus even quoted Moses on this fact in Luke 20:37-38, saying; *"But even Moses showed in the burning bush passage that the dead are raised, when he called the Lord 'the*

God of Abraham, the God of Isaac, and the God of Jacob.' For He is not the God of the dead but of the living, for all live to Him." I believe that is what we experienced at the School of the Seers on Sunday, May 4, 2013. Heaven was invading earth and perhaps some of the great cloud of witnesses were observing the meeting and possible participating in the gathering. I believe it is possible that the great cloud of witnesses participated in much the same manner that Moses participated in the meeting on Mount Tabor. (See Matthew 17:1-3, Mark 9:1-4, and Luke 9:28-30.)

The Great Cloud of Witnesses

You see, as I "looked" into the spirit, I saw this one particular spiritual being and member of the great could of witnesses standing in our midst dressed in what appeared to be a camels' hair vest. There were numerous Godly spiritual beings descending and appearing in the School of the Seers. I was also astonished to "see" and discern that this Godly spiritual being had a tether in his right hand by which he led a dromedary or one-humped camel! I took my right hand and began to touch the vest of this member of the great cloud of witnesses. It seemed that as I articulated the things that I was feeling and seeing, the power and fiery glory of God began to increase in the area around our heavenly visitor! I could touch the snout and nose of the dromedary. The sensation was quite remarkable! It was most unusual to touch the nose and hump of a spiritual camel. Perhaps the camel was symbolic of the Lord releasing supernatural provision to the Body of Christ at this hour?

I invited those in attendance to come forward to exercise their spiritual senses and to feel and discern what I was seeing and feeling. In fact, dozens of people came forward and were able to touch, feel, see, smell, taste, and discern the vest of this Godly spiritual being. What is more, many began to feel the camel and to smell the fragrances of heaven that were being poured out at that moment. The fragrances of roses, frankincense, myrrh, and heavenly aromas were flowing into the room; and many experienced this aromatic and sweet-smelling manifestation. Many people experienced the power of God touch their bodies; and several were slain in the spirit. As one woman touched the area where we believed that spiritual being was standing, she became frozen in place like a statue.

At first she began to say; "I can see the angels of God all around us." Suddenly, as she was speaking, she just went mute and seemed to become frozen in time and space! This same woman stood with her left arm stretched out and in front of her and her eyes opened wide as if gazing at something rather remarkable. She remained "frozen in place" with her eyes wide open for an extended period of time. She remained frozen in place like a statue for perhaps twenty minutes or more. I am not certain. This sign and wonder was similar to manifestations reported during American healing evangelist Maria Woodworth-Etter meetings in the early 1900s. Her meetings also became known for people experiencing trance-like states.

Worshiping in Harmony with God's Angels

These people would later report profound spiritual experiences while in such a state. Many people in the Heaven

113

Touching Earth School of the Seers meetings experienced intense spiritual experiences, and many people began to see into the heavenly realms. Many reported seeing Jesus along with His angels and other members of the great cloud of witnesses in the room. The fragrances of heaven were poured out and many saw and heard the Lord's angelic host worshiping with those gathered that evening near Moravian Falls.

It seemed that many angels were worshiping in harmony with the group of about 320 saints. Many saw the angels as they entered into the meeting through the open heavens. At other moments it seemed that Jesus and Elijah stepped into the room and the power of God was present to release signs and wonders. Many were healed and lots of miracles seemed to occur sovereignly. As time passed the power and the glory of God increased and it seemed that the scriptures from Hebrews 12 literally manifested in the last meeting of the School of the Seers.

In fact, as I had mentioned this passage from Hebrews 12 earlier in the meetings, it seemed that this section of Scripture seemed to initiate the opening of the gates or spiritual portals into the Godly dimensions. Perhaps it is possible that numerous members of the great cloud of witnesses passed between or behind the veil to "attend" the Moravian Falls School of the Seers? Remember, spiritual gates (open heavens) work and open in both directions at times. The following passage summarizes this profound experience.

Hebrews 12:22-29

You have come to Mount Zion and to the city of the living God, the heavenly Jerusalem, to an innumerable company of angels, to the general assembly and church of the firstborn who are registered in heaven, to God the Judge of all, to the spirits of just men made perfect, to Jesus the Mediator of the new covenant, and to the blood of sprinkling that speaks better things than that of Abel. See that you do not refuse Him who speaks. For if they did not escape who refused Him who spoke on earth, much more shall we not escape if we turn away from Him who speaks from heaven, whose voice then shook the earth; but now He has promised, saying, "Yet once more I shake not only the earth, but also heaven." Now this, "Yet once more," indicates the removal of those things that are being shaken, as of things that are made, that the things which cannot be shaken may remain. Therefore, since we are receiving a kingdom which cannot be shaken, let us have grace, by which we may serve God acceptably with reverence and godly fear. For our God is a consuming fire.

Suddenly the power and anointing of God increased to a crescendo; and it truly seemed that the heavenly Jerusalem and an innumerable company of angels, along with the general assembly and church of the firstborn who are registered in heaven, were flooding into the meetings to worship the Lamb of God with those 320 present. His Kingdom had come on earth as it is in Heaven!

Weird Spiritual Creatures

There was no need for anyone to minister as the Kingdom of Heaven had come and the power of God and the Kingdom of Heaven was being released. I stood back in reverential awe as I simply watched what God was doing in the lives and hearts of His people. Healings, miracles, deliverance, and signs and wonders were being released in our midst as the Kingdom of Heaven was invading earth. Even the land seemed to be experiencing deliverance and healing (2 Chronicles 7:14).

During this outpouring the Lord opened my spiritual eyes and I saw what I believe was Mount Zion and the city of the living God come down near the altar. I watched as what I can only describe as a *carousel* of spiritual gates began to appear just in front of me at the altar. By now we had entered into spontaneous worship and adoration of the Lord Jesus Christ. One by one these spiritual gates would open as the carousel of spiritual gates rotated in a counterclockwise fashion. As the carousel would stop in front of me, a spiritual gate would immediately open.

Each time the carousel of spiritual gates rotated, a door or gate into the Godly dimensions would appear and open. Amazingly, just as a carousel at a park would have animals on it, this spiritual carousel had all manner and sorts of angels and other spiritual beings on it! As it would spin, each spiritual gate would stop and open for several moments allowing me to see the Lord of hosts' angelic creatures behind each door. At times they would disembark and maneuver around the room. Sometimes these Godly spiritual creatures just stepped up to the rotating gates or doors and observed us. It seemed they were not released to enter into this realm and they did not pass through the gate or through the veil. However, it seemed that they were very curious to see these weird human creatures in person. I watched this supernatural spectacle unfold before my eyes for nearly an hour. This was not a dream. This was not a trance. This was a full on Technicolor open vision in real time!

I saw various types of Godly angelic beings that appeared. There were also what I assumed to be cherubim and seraphim appear at some of these spiritual gates. I witnessed fiery ones and what may have been elders. There were a plethora of Godly spiritual beings moving into the earthly dimension from the heavenly realms that were opened at the School of the Seers. I discerned hundreds of God's angels descend into the meeting. At times they entered the room to touch and minister to those in attendance.

When this occurred it seemed that the people touched by these Godly angels received something wonderful from the heavenly realms. I made a point of interviewing several of these people later and most of them reported receiving a powerful healing, miracle, or deliverance. All reported being touched by the power of God. Many reported being "set free," and others described how their spiritual eyes were opened to see into the spirit and heavenly dimensions. Many received impartation and reported the activation of the seer anointing in their lives.

I counted an estimated twelve spiritual gates or spiritual doors that opened in the meeting as the carousel rotated around. These twelve gates opened several times over the course of time. I believe that the twelve gates opened twelve times in turn, but I am not positive. Some of the spiritual beings that I saw were most unusual, and I have never seen another spiritual being like them before that time. I saw one spiritual being that appeared to resemble a brain cell that was covered with the phosphorescent glory and hundreds of eyes that seemed to spin continuously.

This unusual spiritual being was about eleven feet in circumference and was roughly circular shaped. The eyes of this member of the Lord's angelic hosts seemed to pierce my very being as its pupils focused upon me. As a result I had to look away, and when I glanced at this spiritual being again it had moved on as the spiritual carousel had shifted again taking us into another Godly dimension of the heavenly realms as a new gate had opened.

The Tangible Power of God

Each time the spiritual carousel would rotate, the glory of God would shift and we would move about into another dimension of glory and of the Godly heavenly realms. I believe that the whole meeting was taken into various places of the heavenly Mount Zion, the New Jerusalem. We had entered into the Kingdom of Heaven, although we were still in the temporal or earthly dimension. Later a member of our team told me that people who were passing the conference center on the way to their rooms in the hotel were affected by the tangible power of God that was being released in the meeting.

One man (who was not a believer) was mightily touched by the power of the tangible glory of God that was hovering in the room. He had to sit down on the couch in the foyer because he was so drunk in the Spirit he could not place one foot in front of the other. His physical body was effected by the power of God in the meeting, and he became like a drunk man (Acts 2:15). This gave our team an opportunity to share the Gospel with this man! He was just staying at the hotel and was not attending the School of the Seers. Although He did not know why, he was weeping because the presence of the Lord as he walked into the "glory zone." The power became so strong at one point that one of the speakers had to be carried out of the meeting. The ushers reported that although this man was slender in build, he was "supernaturally heavy" and they had a difficult time getting him to his room. This was yet another sign and wonder released in our midst!

Many people attending saw Jesus actually step into the meeting at various times and in various places. Others saw and heard God's angelic hosts as they joined us in spontaneous worship. Many reported that they could actually hear the angelic voices, and see the angelic hosts as they were joining the saints as we worshiped the Lord in spirit and in truth. In fact, we were able to capture the worship in digital format and have made the *Throne Room Worship* available as a FREE Mp3 download at the King of Glory Ministries International online store.

During the ministry that night, many people were powerfully touched by the tangible glory and presence of God. No human touched them. No one laid hands upon them. The Kingdom of Heaven and the King of Glory invaded our time and space as spiritual gates opened into the heavenly realms.

People were saved and healed. Miracles abounded. Over sixty people made a decision to serve the Lord with all of their spirit, all of their soul, and all of their bodies. As a result we baptized over sixty people at Moravian Falls. Lives were changed and the Kingdom of God was advanced. You could say that revival visited us for a few days. In my opinion, this was more than the anointing of the Holy Spirit and the hovering or manifestation of the glory of God. This was a release of the end-times power of God, the power of the Father working in tandem with the power of the Holy Spirit as well as the power of the Son.

Secrets Revealed

The power of God is still lingering on me even as I write this on the Day of Atonement, September 14, 2013, at 2:08 a.m. I believe that this incident is a prophetic portrait of what the Lord is releasing at this hour. His people will begin to receive revelation of the hidden and mysterious treasures that can be found in the Kingdom of heaven. God is raising up a royal priesthood according to the order of Melchizedek who will rule and reign in this life. They will have their spiritual eyes and ears open to see and hear the secrets that the Spirit of God is whispering and revealing to His friends at this hour.

This is one aspect of the mantle or the anointing of the royal priesthood according to the order of Melchizedek. It is the grace to see and hear well spiritually. It is the supernatural ability to discern spiritual truths in the same fashion as the Messiah. Then, like Jesus, we will just do those things that we see our Father doing. We will develop our spiritual senses by reason of use. Hebrews 5:14 illustrates this Kingdom dynamic:

"Solid food belongs to those who are of full age, that is, those who by reason of use have their senses exercised to discern both good and evil." That is what happened in the meeting that I have just described.

The Lord is raising up a tribe of believers (His friends, a remnant, mature sons and daughters) who will begin to operate in the powers of the age to come and will be granted a supernatural ability to see, hear, and understand hidden mysteries of the Kingdom of Heaven. At times we will be granted the liberty and grace to step into the heavenly realms. On the other hand, there will be times when the Kingdom of Heaven will invade our space! Discerning these supernatural dynamics of the Kingdom of Heaven is an aspect of the seer anointing.

However this type of supernatural experience is really one aspect of the anointing or the mantle of Melchizedek. In the next chapter I will outline some of the hidden mysteries of the powers of the age to come that will be released by the Lord as this shaking increases.

CHAPTER 13

Accessing Your Heavenly Inheritance

We are stepping into an amazing time on the Lord's calendar. Since 2007 the Lord has been impressing upon me the need to trumpet the message of His royal priesthood. My understanding of this dynamic and this call that God has upon His people was firmly instilled into my spirit when I was launched into the heavenly realms in 2007.

During that experience I was taken up into the heavenly places to sit at the right hand of Jesus (Ephesians 2:6) on a granite bench that was overlooking a magnificent heavenly panoramic vista. It was during that visit to the heavenly places that the Lord released me to begin to teach and preach about the seer anointing. Later in 2010, the Lord visited me on the Day of Atonement and gave me further revelation concerning the eminent manifestation of the royal priesthood according to the order of Melchizedek.

Again, I believe that the Lord is releasing all of His people to minister and walk in this type of heavenly calling and anointing. As royal priests according to the order of Melchizedek, God's people will begin to have a much greater level of discernment. They will begin to see and hear what the Lord is releasing in the heavenly realms. Then, like the Lord Jesus Christ, they will do those things that they see their Father doing.

This is an aspect of the seer realm or the seer anointing. It is possible that in the past this supernatural ability or gift was only available to "chosen vessels." I believe that this was certainly true during the Old Testament. However, in this dispensation of grace, or after the New Testament and its new covenant was released, this promise is now for "whosoever."

We see these wonderful promises in the Book of Hebrews, chapters 7 and 8, and it is culminated in Hebrews chapter 12—*Jesus is the Mediator of the new covenant.* As we have learned, one aspect of this anointing or privilege is the ability to literally ascend into the heavenly realms to access or tap into the heavenly power of God that resides there at the right hand of the Father.

When we develop our spiritual senses by reason of use and learn to walk as mature sons and daughters of God, we can begin to step into this realm. In subsequent chapters I want to share these kinds of testimonies with you. I believe they can be the spirit of prophesy for many of you reading this right now. I believe that the Lord's heart for His people is to learn to literally come boldly to the throne of grace to find help in their time of need as described in Hebrews 4:16: "*Let us therefore come boldly to the throne of grace, that we may obtain mercy and find grace to help in time of need.*"

This scripture is not just some flowery alliteration, but it is a reality for those who love the Lord with all of their heart, all of their soul, and all of their mind at this hour. The God of the universe is literally calling His friends to come up to His throne. Since 2001 I have had the privilege of experiencing these kinds of supernatural encounters with the Kingdom of Heaven. I have written about many of these throne-room experiences where I was taken up into the heavenly realms extensively in the trilogy of books, *The Reality of Angelic Ministry Today,*" books 1, 2, and 3. I have also written about other supernatural encounters in the book *The Sword of the Lord & The Rest of the Lord.*

The response to these books has been amazing and very encouraging. We have received hundreds of emails and letters from all over the world from people who have had similar experiences. In addition to this, it is apparent to me that there is now an acceleration of these kinds of heavenly encounters. More and more people are having angelic encounters or are being taken up into the heavenly realms at this hour. It is well document that the Lord Jesus is even appearing to Muslim clerics, and there are many who have received the Lord as Messiah or Savior; and these forerunners are now ministering or preaching the Gospel of the Kingdom.

During the dozens of heavenly experiences that are documented in the books that I have mentioned, I have been allowed to see or to approach the throne in the heavenly realms occasionally. I believe that there are two or more thrones in heaven. One is a throne of Mercy and Judgment. I also believe that there is also a throne which I refer to as the throne of the Ancient of Days. In this place we are allowed, at times and as the Lord wills, to present our case before the Creator of heaven and earth.

Here are a few scriptural examples of these kinds of throne-room encounters.

I believe that this scripture in Daniel 7:9-10 describes the throne of the Ancient of Days:

> *I watched till thrones were put in place, And the Ancient of Days was seated; His garment was white as snow, And the hair of His head was like pure wool. His throne was a fiery flame, Its wheels a burning fire; A fiery stream issued And came forth from before Him. A thousand thousands ministered to Him; Ten thousand times ten thousand stood before Him. The court was seated, And the books were opened.*

Zechariah 3:1-8 also describes this throne of God:

> *Then he showed me Joshua the high priest standing before the Angel of the LORD, and Satan standing at his right hand to oppose him. And the LORD said to Satan, "The LORD rebuke you, Satan! The LORD who has chosen Jerusalem rebuke you! Is this not a brand plucked from the fire?" Now Joshua was clothed with filthy garments, and was standing before the Angel. Then He answered and spoke to those who stood before Him, saying, "Take away the filthy garments from him." And to him He said, "See, I have removed your iniquity from you, and I will clothe you with rich robes." And I said, "Let them put a clean turban on his head." So they put a clean turban*

on his head, and they put the clothes on him. And the Angel of the LORD stood by. Then the Angel of the LORD admonished "Thus says the LORD of hosts: 'If you will walk in My ways, And if you will keep My command, Then you shall also judge My house, And likewise have charge of My courts; I will give you places to walk Among these who stand here. Hear, O Joshua, the high priest, You and your companions who sit before you, For they are a wondrous sign; For behold, I am bringing forth My Servant the BRANCH.'"

I believe that the prophet Isaiah also was granted the privilege to ascend into the heavenly realms to stand before the throne of the Lord. Of course Isaiah was also a seer prophet. Daniel was also a seer prophet. In other words, Isaiah and Daniel were prototypes or foreshadows of the royal priesthood according to the order of Melchizedek that the Lord is raising up at this hour. You are called by God to be a seer at this hour.

Look at Isaiah 6:1-10:

In the year that King Uzziah died, I saw the Lord sitting on a throne, high and lifted up, and the train of His robe filled the temple. Above it stood seraphim; each one had six wings: with two he covered his face, with two he covered his feet, and with two he flew. And one cried to another and said: "Holy, holy, holy is the LORD of hosts; The whole earth is full of His glory!" And the posts of the door were shaken by the voice of him who cried out, and the house was filled with smoke. So I said: "Woe is me, for I am undone! Because I am a man of unclean lips, And

I dwell in the midst of a people of unclean lips; For my eyes have seen the King, The LORD of hosts." Then one of the seraphim flew to me, having in his hand a live coal which he had taken with the tongs from the altar. And he touched my mouth with it, and said: "Behold, this has touched your lips; Your iniquity is taken away, And your sin purged." Also I heard the voice of the Lord, saying: "Whom shall I send, And who will go for Us?" Then I said, "Here am I! Send me." And He said, "Go, and tell this people: 'Keep on hearing, but do not understand; Keep on seeing but do not perceive.' Make the heart of this people dull, And their ears heavy, And shut their eyes; Lest they see with their eyes, And hear with their ears, And understand with their heart, And return and be healed."

There are many other examples in the scriptures as well. I have not even mentioned John the Revelator and the Book of Revelation, which, by the way, is another excellent example of this kind of supernatural experience. The Book of Revelation is a wonderful example of a throne-room encounter. I would like to suggest that you study it. Meditate upon the twenty-two chapters therein as they can be an excellent prophetic promise for you! There are thirty-three references to the throne of God in the Book of Revelation alone!

Interestingly enough, the number thirty-three has a wonderful prophetic significance. The number thirty-three is connected to the promises and covenants of God. Remember that the Lord has given us a new and better covenant. Thirty-three is connected to the promise that God gave Noah. The son of promise, Isaac, was born to Abraham immediately after his name was mentioned the thirty-third time. There are many other correlations that are too numerous to mention here.

However, I believe that we have the promise from the Lord that we can literally ascend to the throne of mercy and grace at this hour. If you are a "whosoever," you can approach the throne of God to obtain mercy and find grace and help in your time of need. Having said all of this, allow me to encourage you that approaching the throne of God, or entering into the throne room, can be a daunting experience!

The first time that the Lord took me into the presence of the Father as He sat upon the throne, I thought that I was going to die. The absolute reverential fear and knowledge of the Lord nearly consumed me, and I sought to crawl under the marble tiles of the throne room. If there had not been four of God's angels standing by my side holding me up, I would have surely fainted. I felt very much like the prophet Isaiah when he said, "*I am a man of unclean lips, and I dwell in the midst of a people of unclean lips; yet my eyes have seen the King, The LORD of hosts.*"

However, I believe that the scriptures in Revelation chapter 1 are a promise for you!

Revelation 1:1-6

The Revelation of Jesus Christ, which God gave Him to show His servants—things which must shortly take place. And He sent and signified it by His angel to His servant John, who bore witness to the word of God, and to the testimony of Jesus Christ, to all things that he saw. Blessed is he who reads and those who hear the words of this prophecy, and keep those things which are written in it; for the time is near. John, to the seven churches which are in Asia: Grace to you and peace from Him who is and who was and who is to come, and from the seven Spirits who are before His throne, and from Jesus Christ, the faithful witness, the firstborn from the dead, and the ruler over the kings of the earth. To Him who loved us and washed us from our sins in His own blood, and has made us kings and priests to His God and Father, to Him be glory and dominion forever and ever. Amen.

As I stated earlier, I believe that this is what God placed you upon the earth for. You are called to be a king and priest to our God and Father! How? Through the cleansing, atoning blood of Jesus Christ of Nazareth. The Savior who loved each of us so much that He washed us from our sins, with His blood, to make you and me kings and priests to our God and Father.

This promise is not for the millennial reign, this is a promise for you now. The Father is seated in the heavenly realms; and in order for you and me to minister to the Father, we must go where He is. We must boldly go where few men have gone before. We must ascend into the heavenly dimensions and stand before the throne of our Papa, our God and our Father.

As I stated earlier, the first time I came into the throne room and stood near the throne of the Father, I was certain I was about to die. I felt very much like the Israelites at Mount Horeb (Exodus 20:18-19). However, I know from experience that you can approach the Father. You can learn to develop your spiritual senses by reason of use to develop and increase your ability to stand in the glory. You can minister to God the Father in the heavenly realms. In fact, you can speak to the Father as a man speaks to a friend.

In the next chapter I share a wonderful testimony of how God is speaking face-to-face with His friends at this hour. By the grace of God I was allowed to experience an amazing throne-room encounter with the Father. I also believe that the Creator of the universe has opened the doors or gates of the heavenly dimensions for you to have similar throne-room experiences. The Father is saying, "Come up here!" Papa wants to talk to you face-to-face as a man does with a friend. Elohim, the Creator of heavens and earth, wishes to release supernatural blessings and favor into your life as you learn to exercise your spiritual senses and access the throne room and the realms of heaven at this hour. In my opinion, this is one of the hidden mysteries of the powers of the age to come. You can visit the Father's throne and receive a measure of the power of the Kingdom that is being released to God's friends there in the heavenly realms.

CHAPTER 14

Accessing the Father's Throne

On Saturday, July 20, 2014, at 4:38 p.m., I had such an experience! We were hosting one of the first Summer Schools of the Supernatural here near Moravian Falls. I had been teaching messages about our role as royal priests according to the order of Melchizedek. In my spirit I felt the need to fast before the evening service and seek the Lord for guidance for the ministry time for the Sunday evening service (which was our graduation service or impartation service). Kathy traveled to our little cabin to feed our puppy, Annie. The ministry team and delegates went to have dinner or to seek the Lord on their own.

I slipped out of the meeting to invest the next two hours in soaking prayer. It was my desire to rest in the glory and presence of the Lord. The Lord had spoken to me about the importance of this kind of prayer on the Day of Atonement in 2012. The Lord said, *"When you learn to rest in My glory, My glory will begin to rest upon you."* I had no idea how real those words would turn out to be that day!

I had been seeking to rest in the Lord's glory for a season, and there have been times when His glory will come in great power in my little prayer room in our little cabin. Let me say to you, one moment in the legitimate glory of God can transform your life! I call this a supernatural exchange. I really believe that this dynamic, learning to rest in God's glory, can transform your life too. If you would like to learn more about this supernatural exchange get the "Transformation Glory" and "Cultivating the Glory" teachings from our bookstore.

The Ancient of Days

One of the things I have learned is that the glory of God can come upon or rest upon you at any time or in any place. So on the Saturday evening at the Summer School of the Supernatural, I was really seeking to rest my voice and my physical body. I was not expecting anything extraordinary to transpire in the time between the sessions. However, when I entered the room there was an unusual silence and lingering holiness present. I brushed my teeth, and bowed my knees at the side of the bed. I prayed the apostolic prayer from Ephesians 3:14-21.

Then I lay down on the bed and began to rest in Him. I was not praying. I was not asking to be taken into heaven. I just wanted to experience His presence. I just wanted to experience His glory. I just wanted to be with Him. I just wanted to rest in His glory for a couple of hours. After a few minutes I brought my mind into subjection to my recreated spirit. I took my thoughts captive and determined in my spirit that I was going to focus on the Lord and worship Papa.

Suddenly a holy swoosh filled the room, and it seemed as if I was being taken into another dimension. It was not so much that I was going up, but I felt that the Kingdom was coming down. I closed my eyes and began to relax. I began to luxuriate in the power and the glory of God that was filling the place. After a while I realized that I had ascended. I was no longer in the hotel. I was in the heavenly realms. I opened my eyes to look and found that I was at the throne of the Ancient of Days.

My first instinct was to tense up, as I had experienced great trepidation and the reverential fear of the Lord in this place before. (The initial experience of coming before the throne of God is outlined in *Dancing with Angels 2*, chapter 14, "Anointed to Reign as Priests and Prophets.") However, in this instance I had a supernatural peace. There was no one there to accuse me, and the Lord Jesus was standing to my left. Jesus was dressed in His priestly garments, and He was speaking to the Father in a language that I did not comprehend. Somehow I knew that Jesus was speaking to the Father on my behalf, as my advocate.

I stood there for an instant and watched this scenario unfold as if I was an innocent child. I looked at my surroundings. At that moment I witnessed Jesus Christ ministering as the Royal Priest according to the order of Melchizedek. I looked at the innumerable gathering of angelic and other spiritual beings and what may well have been the great cloud of witnesses (by the way, these two are different types of spiritual beings from the heavenly realms). A supernatural peace that surpassed my ability to understand filled my spirit. By now I was lost in the heavenly realms. I looked at my feet to see that they were bare.

I was standing on beautiful white marble, and its texture was cool and comforting on the soles of my feet. I had a beautiful white robe on, and it was reflecting the glorious colors that seemed to emanate from and around the Father's throne.

I realized that this was a place of victory and grace and I need not be fearful on this visit. As this thought bubbled up within my spirit, a smile filled my face and the angelic being standing next to me also began to smiled broadly. I became lost in my thoughts and time and space seemed to stop for that moment. Nearby was the sea of glass like crystal. I always like to go there as it is a place of revelation and refreshing. But today I found myself lost in paradise and eternity at the foot of the throne of the Ancient of Days. Worship filled the air around the throne. Glory vaulted through the throne room and the lights of heaven reflected off of the crystal structures that rose high into the heavens around the Father's throne. I believe that these are balconies, and they were populated with heavenly hosts. There was beautiful singing and worship music that seemed to be coming from these balconies filling the throne room. There appeared to be both angelic beings and those who had human form; perhaps members of the great cloud of witnesses? Again, I am not sure.

Suddenly none of these things seemed to matter. The Summer School of the Supernatural was but a distant memory. My prayers, not important. Being in the presence of the Father, amazing. I felt like a small two- or three-year-old boy. There was no way that I could comprehend the things that take place there. Nor was I the least bit concerned at out my inability to understand these heavenly dynamics and workings of the throne room at all. It did not matter. I was just happy to be near my Father with Jesus ministering to the Father on my behalf as my Advocate. Later the scripture from 1 John 2:1 filled my heart: "*My little children, these things I write to you, so that you may not sin. And if anyone sins, we have an Advocate with the Father, Jesus Christ the righteous.*"

That evening I was like a little child. I had no cares; because I knew that as long as I was in the presence of my Father, no one could harm me in any way. This understanding brought me great peace and joy. Without realizing it I began to worship the Father along with the innumerable angelic host present. Glancing to my left I noticed that the angel at my side appeared to be a little stunned as he was gazing at me with his mouth agape and his eyes open wide. I looked into this angel's eyes and smiled at him and sung a little louder. At that moment I was surprised that I knew the lyrics to the song, as it was not being sung in English. This surprised me and perhaps was the reason for the angel's wonderment.

I closed my eyes and worshiped some more, and time seemed to pass without end. After a long while I realized that it was silent around the throne, save for me and an unusual buzzing sound. I immediately stopped singing and opened my eyes to see what appeared to be seraphim zooming in circular patterns around the Father's throne in acrobatic maneuvers. The glory of God was being cast off of their wings in every direction. The glory seemed to radiate from their wings spreading instantly into every crevice of the throne room sending phosphorescent glory and heavenly light everywhere. These heavenly colors seemed to multiply when they reflected off of the crystal materials all around the throne room. I watched this spectacle for an instant, and for just the tiniest nanosecond there was silence in heaven. I could have watched that supernatural display of God's glory for eternity!

Wonderment and Love

The silence greatly surprised me, and I shifted my gaze to look at the Father's throne. As I shifted my gaze, I noticed that Jesus had stopped talking. He was now looking at me. Then Jesus shifted His eyes from me to look up at the Father. As the Lord was turning His head, I heard these words: *"Come up here!"* The throne room shook as those words thundered through the heavenly realms. In that instant I wondered who the Father was speaking to. I followed Jesus' gaze to look at the Father's throne again. For an instant the clouds parted and I saw the Father's hands move out from the glory. I heard the words a second time: *"Come up here!"*

The words were filled with wonderment and love. There was a great peace that rode upon the words the Father was speaking at that second. Once more I wondered who the Father was speaking to; and as this thought entered my mind, I saw His hands reaching down in my direction and I realized that the Father was talking to me! Before I could even think, the hand of God scooped me up and soon I was gently cupped in the hands of the Father. I did not see the Father's face, but He gently took me from the place that I was standing worshipping before the throne into the very glory of God. The Love of the Father enveloped me in a way that I have never experienced before. This was resting in His glory!

Somehow I knew that the Father was looking at me very carefully and studying me with great curiosity and amazement. The Creator was looking at the creature in wonderment! I was reminded of Psalm 8:4: *"What is man that You are mindful of him, And the son of man that You visit him?"* The Father was meticulously scrutinizing every cell of my being as He cradled me in His hands like I was a newborn baby. He said; *"I am glad that you are here. "*

An eternity seemed to pass as the Father held me near His chest or perhaps His bosom. The glory and power of the Father penetrated every fiber of my being. After a while He spoke again and said,

> *I like the fact that when you pray to Me, you come to My throne of mercy and grace. You do not come to judge or to ask for judgments to come upon others. You ask Me for mercy and grace. I like that. My throne is a place of mercy and grace. Always remember to come to My throne and ask for mercy and grace. That is My heart. Pray My heart. Remember that it is My goodness that leads men to repentance.*

See Romans 2.

The Power of Papa

At that moment I was truly undone. The words the Father spoke thundered through the throne room, and they pierced my very heart. Tears began to pour from my eyes. (I would like to pontificate that it is possible my tears were flowing in the hotel and not in the heavenly realms.) I was in shock. The

Father had just told me that He liked the way that I prayed. He is a God of mercy and grace and the thoughts came into my spirit: *"Thank You, Lord, for You are good and Your mercy endures forever."*

The Father cradled me in His massive and mighty hands for another few moments, and I thought of what Jesus said in John 10:27-29:

> *My sheep hear My voice, and I know them, and they follow Me. And I give them eternal life, and they shall never perish; neither shall anyone snatch them out of My hand. My Father, who has given them to Me, is greater than all; and no one is able to snatch them out of My Father's hand.*

At that instant I had an unshakable understanding that nothing can snatch one of God's people from His mighty hand. No one could snatch me from the Father's hand at that moment. This was truly the secret place of the Most High!

At His hand we live in the secret place (Psalm 91). In His right hand are pleasures for evermore (Psalm 16:11). The glory of the Father rolled over and through every fiber of my spirit, soul, and body for what seemed like an eternity! I was lost somewhere in the spirit. I was being refreshed. I was being renewed. I was being ministered to by the Father of glory (Ephesians 1:17-23)! It seemed that time without end seemed to pass. I rested in His glory for what seemed like an eternity. It felt like days, but it must have only been a few moments in the heavenly realms. I experienced the power of Papa's love.

The Resonance of Heaven

Finally I was jarred back to my senses by the voice of the Father once more. He said; "*You are welcome to come back here any time you like.*" I realized that the Father was lifting me up to look at me one last time as He was speaking these words. I somehow knew that He was smiling at me although I could not see His face as the glory around Him is just too intense. I was placed back beside Jesus at the foot of the throne of the Ancient of Days.

I was stunned; and as I started to slump to the marble floor, four angelic beings hurried to my side and held me up by my arms. My entire being seemed to vibrate and resonate at a higher frequency. I glanced to my left to see the Lord Jesus and He was beaming broadly, smiling at me with assurance and what seemed to be great satisfaction. I took one last look at the glory as it swirled about surrounding the Father. The Father's mighty hands disappeared, slipping easily back inside of the intense glory around His throne. I now believe that the glory that is hovering around the Throne of the Father is the Holy Spirit.

I saw several seraphim buzzing through the glory clouds again dispersing the glory throughout the throne room in all directions simultaneously. I believe that these seraphim are not angels, but rather they are part of God's heavenly hosts; members of the Lord of Host's great end-time army. In hindsight I think there were four in attendance at the Father's throne, but I am not certain.

Then I was aware of the worship again, the words *holy, holy, holy* seemed to thunder around the throne! It seemed as all of heaven was shaking at that instant. Heaven was vibrating at a very high frequency, and the throne room seemed to be resonating like a tuning fork at that instant. I assume it was the grace of God that allowed me to discern this harmonic vibration and resonance of heaven at that moment. Heaven seemed to vibrate and shake at a perfect pitch and harmonic frequency. Suddenly I realized that God will once more shake the heavens and the earth at this hour! I realized that I was living Hebrews 12:26 when God's *"voice then shook the earth; but now He has promised, saying, 'Yet once more I shake not only the earth, but heaven also.'"*

I closed my eyes and joined in with the angelic hosts and great cloud of witnesses singing, "Holy, holy, holy." When I opened my eyes, I was back in the hotel singing in tongues, yet I know that I was saying, "Holy, holy, holy." Apparently I had been singing in tongues for a long time, as nearly two hours had passed. A purple glory cloud hovered about four feet off of the floor and the fragrances of fire and roses permeated the air. Tears flowed from my eyes, and I continued to worship with those around the throne. "Holy, holy, holy is the Lord God Almighty."

Revelation 4:8

The four living creatures, each having six wings, were full of eyes around and within. And they do not rest day or night, saying: "Holy, holy, holy, Lord God Almighty, Who was and is and is to come!"

I looked at the clock later to check the time, as I was needed in the school at 7 p.m. However, I am also certain that I was in the throne room and in the hands of the Father for a day or two. It is not the time that we think it is! I felt rested, refreshed, and ready for the evening meetings. After a few more minutes, I got up to brush my teeth. I leaned upon the sink and looked at myself in the mirror. I was shocked to discover that my hair had started to turn grey. In fact, it appeared that I had about 25 percent more silver in my hair! When I stepped into the meeting someone even commented on my "new look." "When did your hair start to turn grey," they asked? I just smiled and said, "Recently; very recently!" Another person stated offhandedly that I looked like my "face was shining." Both may have well been right!

We are currently living at a God-ordained moment of time when the Creator of the heavens and the earth is seeking the true sons and daughters of God to arise. The Lord is releasing hidden mysteries and supernatural secrets to His children at this hour. There is a grace from heaven to step into hidden and mysterious aspects of Christ's Kingdom available to you today that, I believe, was not open to the sons of man before. The Lord is releasing the Key of David and the hidden keys to the Kingdom of Heaven to His children at this hour.

I believe that what Jesus said in Matthew 16:19, has a much broader interpretation than we can fathom. The Lord said, "*I will give you the keys of the Kingdom of Heaven, and whatever you bind on earth will be bound in heaven, and whatever you loose on earth will be loosed in heaven.*" In the next chapters we will begin to explore these hidden mysteries of the Kingdom and develop your faith to believe for God to release the powers of the ages to come to your life.

CHAPTER 15

The Fellowship of the Hidden Mysteries of the Kingdom of Heaven

Jesus taught the parable of the sower in three of the Synoptic Gospels (Matthew 13, Mark 4, and Luke 8). This parable is one of the few parables of Jesus that the Lord gives us an interpretation or explanation. By the grace of God, I have had Jesus speak to me numerous times. And many times He speaks to me, at least, in parables. Often when I look back on things that the Lord has told me about my life or ministry or events that are yet to take place, I realize that Jesus continues to teach and speak in parables to His children today.

At this point let me say that you should consider this carefully, as this is my opinion and may be construed by many theologians as "extra-biblical." In fact, there is no doubt that my visitations and the encounters that I have lived through are certainly construed by some to be extra-biblical. However, that does not invalidate them in the realm of the Kingdom of Heaven. But, it may mean that you need to seek the Lord for yourself about these theories the Lord has birthed in my heart. In fact, I encourage you to seek the Lord and study the Scriptures for yourself about anything that I have said or that I have written that may seem extra-biblical. You are free to disagree with me and even publish your own manuscript on the subject if you so wish.

This is what I believe. We (Christians) don't always believe the Bible or the Canon of Scripture. Often we believe *what we have been told* that the Bible says, or we believe *what others have taught us* that the scriptures mean. But many times we do not believe the Gospel or the truth of the Scriptures. Many of us have an inaccurate understanding of the truth. We do not fully comprehend the enormity and totality of the Gospel of Jesus Christ. In fact, for us to say today that we fully comprehend and know every idiosyncrasy that is in the Scriptures that make up the Gospel is the height of spiritual pride and quite possibly a religious spirit and/or a mental stronghold.

Remember what Jesus said in Matthew 11:25-27:

> *I thank You, Father, Lord of heaven and earth, that You have hidden these things from the wise and prudent and have revealed them to babes. Even so, Father, for so it seemed good in Your sight. All things have been delivered to Me by My Father, and no one knows the Son except the Father. Nor does anyone know the Father except the Son, and the one to whom the Son wills to reveal Him.*

Jesus also revealed this aspect of the Father's heart (concerning how the Kingdom of Heaven contains mysteries and secrets) in Luke 12: 31-32: *"But seek the kingdom of God, and all these things shall be added to you. Do not fear, little flock, for it is your Father's good pleasure to give you the kingdom."* The Father takes great pleasure when we come to Him as a little child, doubting nothing, but believing in God's love, grace, and power to work in our lives as babes. The Apostle Paul also understood that childlike faith was pivotal to understanding the weightier matters of the Kingdom of Heaven. It is the Father's good pleasure to give His children the hidden and mysterious treasures of the Kingdom. If we believe that we understand all of the mysteries of the Kingdom of Heaven, then I believe that God will be hesitant to reveal more of His mysteries to us.

In fact, I am certain that we, as the Body of Christ, actually know little or nothing of the magnificent truths and glories of the Kingdom of our God and His Christ. There are hidden mysteries and revelatory knowledge that are available to each of us at this hour. We will invest eternity searching out the unsearchable riches of Christ. Unfortunately many of our hearts are dull, our ears are heavy, and our eyes are shut or spiritually blind. But it is God's heart for us to see with our eyes, and hear with our ears, and understand with our heart. Then perhaps God's people will return to the Lord in fullness and be healed. In other words, we will be able to see, hear, and comprehend the hidden and mysterious secrets of the Kingdom of Heaven.

The Treasures of His Kingdom

There is so much more that the Lord wishes for His people to hear and to see. I believe that there are so many more hidden

147

mysteries and revelatory knowledge that the Father desperately desires for His people to walk in. God longs for the true sons and daughters of the Kingdom to arise and to walk in the fullness of the power of the Holy Spirit and in the power of the ages to come (Ephesians 1:21). In fact, I believe that the Lord is releasing these hidden and mysterious treasures of His Kingdom to His children at this hour. The Apostle Paul received his supernatural understanding and revelation through Jesus Christ during his personal supernatural discipleship. Though, Paul was never able to fully teach these hidden mysteries openly to the Body of Christ in the first century.

Why? I believe that the Lord would not release the Apostle Paul to share and teach the amazing revelations and experiences that were made know to him by the Lord Jesus Christ. However, Paul hints of these in the Ephesians 3. I also believe this because I have seen Epistles written by the Apostle Paul in the heavenly realms—things so deep and mysterious that God would not allow him to speak or teach them in his day. However, I believe that the Lord is raising up an end-time army who will be given the keys to these kinds of secrets and supernatural hidden mysteries.

God will begin to empower His friends to walk and minister in the powers of the age to come! For we are at an eternal crossroads when the Lord will begin to raise up and release people who will be enlightened and who will taste of the heavenly gift and of the eternal power of the Son, the Holy Spirit, and the power of the Father. This chosen generation of royal priests according to the order of Melchizedek will have the supernatural God-given revelation of the word of God and will be granted the supernatural grace to unlock the hidden mysteries of the scriptures. They will know the good word of God and the powers of the age to come. The Holy Spirit will give them supernatural revelation from the word of God, what is commonly referred to as the Canon of Scripture.

These holy friends of God will learn that it is possible for them to come boldly to the throne of mercy and grace. They will freely enter the presence of God behind the veil, or spiritual realms. These royal priests according to the order of Melchizedek will follow the Messiah, Jesus Christ of Nazareth, into the very presence of Almighty God to receive and understand hidden and mysterious truths. They will follow the example of the Forerunner, who has entered into the heavenly realms for us, so that we too can become priests to our God and Father forever according to the order of Melchizedek (Hebrews 6:20; Revelation 1:6). We too can expect to receive power and revelation at the right hand of the Father in the heavenly realms.

The Apostle Paul understood this heavenly dynamic. Paul had this revelation; yet I believe that the Lord withheld Him from sharing it in fullness, though we see that the apostle hints of this Kingdom dynamic and hidden mystery writing cryptically about it in Ephesians chapter 3. We see some amazing truth here in Ephesians 3:1-13. Let's dissect this passage briefly:

Verses 1 and 2 tell us:

For this reason I, Paul, the prisoner of Christ Jesus for you Gentiles—if indeed you have heard of the dispensation of the grace of God which was given to me for you.

What dispensation of grace is Paul referring to? I believe that Paul is referring to the revelatory knowledge that Jesus Christ imparted to him personally in the heavenly realms and or during earthly visitations of the resurrected Messiah. We see this spelled out in the next few verses.

Verses 3 and 4 say:

> *How that by revelation He [Jesus] made known to me the mystery" (as I have briefly written already, by which, when you read, you may understand my knowledge in the mystery of Christ).*

Question for you? Where are these letters referred to in this last scripture? Was Paul referring to the other Epistles that he authored that are in the Bible? The answer is, possibly. However, I also believe that I have seen in the heavenly realms other letters or epistles written by Paul that were not included in the Canon of Scripture. So, there may well be a lot more revelation that has been written by the Apostle Paul concerning the hidden mysteries and secrets of the Kingdom of Heaven. This is my humble opinion.

Verses 5-13 illustrate this idea:

> *Which in other ages was not made known to the sons of men, as it has now been revealed by the Spirit to His holy apostles and prophets: that the Gentiles should be fellow heirs, of the same body, and partakers of His promise in Christ through the gospel, of which I became a minister according to the gift of the grace of God given to me by the effective working of His power. To me, who am less*

than the least of all the saints, this grace was given, that I should preach among the Gentiles the unsearchable riches of Christ, and to make all see what is the fellowship of the mystery, which from the beginning of the ages has been hidden in God who created all things through Jesus Christ; to the intent that now the manifold wisdom of God might be made known by the church to the principalities and powers in the heavenly places, according to the eternal purpose which He accomplished in Christ Jesus our Lord, in whom we have boldness and access with confidence through faith in Him. Therefore I ask that you do not lose heart at my tribulations for you, which is your glory.

God-Ordained Release of Heavenly Visitations

I believe that God also wishes to visit you at this hour in a similar manner that He visited the Apostle Paul when he was just Saul. God wants to empower you with His Spirit and take you into the weightier matters of His Kingdom and to understand the manifold wisdom of God. The Father has many hidden mysteries and secret treasures that He desires for you to uncover at this God-ordained hour. It is truly the Father's good pleasure to give you the secrets and mysterious things of His Kingdom. I believe that it is the heart of the Lord Jesus Christ to impart some spiritual gifts to you personally in the heavenly realms (Romans 1:11; Ephesians 3:3-4).

I believe that God is looking for the least likely. The Spirit of the Living God is actively searching for those who would be considered foolish according to the world's wisdom and intellectual knowledge; because the Lord will begin to do great and mighty exploits through the least of these (Daniel 11:32; Matthew 25:45). God will begin to raise up many of the least likely to release mighty revivals to win the great harvest as the Father begins to accelerate the God-ordained release of earthly visitations of the Lord Jesus Christ. These mature sons and daughters will be given incredible wisdom, revelation, and unreserved understanding of the manifold wisdom of the Most High God.

In addition to this, the heavenly realms will also begin to invade our spheres of influence as the day of the Lord's triumphant return draws near, and there will be a marked increase of the visitations of the great cloud of witnesses upon the earth. Remember what Jesus said, speaking of the Father, in Luke 20:38: "*For He is not the God of the dead but of the living, for all live to Him.*" I believe that the veil between the heavenly dimensions and the earthly realms has become thin and more porous that at any moment in the history of earth since the fall (save for the Garden of Eden prior to the fall).

What Is the Cost?

At this hour many of those who position themselves to receive will have Christ appear to them. Just "believe to receive." The Lord will visit them much like He visited Saul in Acts 9, who later became Paul when he was filled with the Holy Spirit. Much like he visited me on November 25, 2001. God found in me, the vilest of sinners, something that He could use. What did the Lord find in me? He found someone who was broken by the world's standards. He found someone who was humbled and willing to receive His word as the Gospel and as the truth. He found someone with childlike faith. He found someone who knew that there was more to the Kingdom of God than sitting in a pew on Sundays. He found someone who was hungry for more of Him. He found someone who would just say, "Yes. Lord," no matter how absurd the request was. In me He found a willing and broken vessel. He found someone willing to be obedient to His voice and His leadings no matter what the cost. He found someone with a broken and contrite heart (Psalm 34:18; Isaiah 57:15).

How about you? Are you ready to have the Creator of the heavens and the earth visit you? Are you ready to have your heavenly Father give you the Kingdom of Heaven and all of the secrets and hidden mysteries that are concealed within? I believe that the God of the universe is calling out your name. The Lord is seeking to reveal to you the fellowship of the mysteries concealed within His Kingdom. Are you willing? Are you broken (Mark 8:34)? Are you available?

God is seeking friends to whom He can reveal the hidden mysteries, which have been hidden in God in Christ from the beginning of the ages. Think of this amazing and incredible truth! The Creator of the heavens and the earth, who created all things through Jesus Christ, is seeking friends to whom He can reveal hidden mysteries so that the manifold wisdom of God might be made known by the church to the principalities and powers in the heavenly places. Is it not marvelous that the Lord is calling you to be an essential part of releasing the revelation of the hidden mysterious secrets of heaven to the whole world according to the eternal purpose which He accomplished in Christ Jesus our Lord and Savior?

I find it amazing that God would use me; and perhaps you may also find it astonishing that God wants to use you as well. But He does. The Father wants to give you the hidden and secret things in His Kingdom. He wants you to walk as mature sons and daughters of the Most High God. He wants to empower you to not only walk in, but also to understand the power of the ages to come; *"For the earnest expectation of the creation eagerly waits for the revealing of the sons of God"* (Romans 8:19). The Father is calling you to *arise!*

The Apostle Paul spells out this spiritual truth yet again in 1 Corinthians 1:27-31:

> *God has chosen the foolish things of the world to put to shame the wise, and God has chosen the weak things of the world to put to shame the things which are mighty; and the base things of the world and the things which are despised God has chosen, and the things which are not, to bring to nothing the things that are, that no flesh should glory in His presence. But of Him you are in Christ Jesus, who became for us wisdom from God--and righteousness and sanctification and redemption that, as it is written, "He who glories, let him glory in the LORD."*

God is so amazing! He is looking for you! The Father wishes to give you supernatural treasure and to give you approval to operate in the powers of the ages to come. *Arise!*

Getting back to the parable of the sower, I want to share a revelation that the Lord gave to me in the heavenly realms.

The parables of Jesus are still active. The Lord Jesus Christ still speaks in parables today. In fact, the parable of the sower in Luke 8 is a parable within a parable. In other words, there is hidden revelation to this day in the scriptures, and I believe that this is especially true for Luke 8:10: *"And Jesus said, 'To you it has been given to know the mysteries of the Kingdom of God, but to the rest it is given in parables, that "Seeing they may not see, And hearing they may not understand."'"*

That is the day and hour that we are living in! It *HAS* been given to you to know the hidden and mysterious secrets that are obscured and buried in the Kingdom of Heaven. God *is* releasing revelatory understanding to His people at this hour. For some people that revelation will come from the word of God or the Canon of Scripture. For others Jesus will begin to visit them and reveal to them secrets, revelations, and understanding of hidden mysteries in the same manner that He did when He visited the Apostle Paul. Perhaps God will make known to you the knowledge of the mysteries hidden in Christ. Hidden mysteries and revelations that in other ages were not made known to the sons of men are *now* being revealed to God's friends today.

We are entering into that God-ordained era and eternal crossroads when the Creator will begin to reveal the deep and hidden mysteries of the Kingdom of Heaven. The mysterious treasures and the powers of the age to come will soon be revealed to the world through the people of God as they are given by His Spirit to His friends, (a royal priesthood). I call these people (friends of God) a holy people, a royal priesthood according to the order of Melchizedek. The mature sons and daughters of the Most High God are arising! Hallelujah! In the next chapter I want to look in more detail at what I believe is the imminent release of the powers of the age to come. This is not necessarily the power of the Holy Spirit, but rather the power of the whole Trinity. God will shake every nation of the earth with this power and with true revival to usher in the great last day's harvest (Joel 3:13; Matthew 9:37-38).

CHAPTER 16

The Glory of God and the Law of Observation

I am no longer concerned about time the way that I used to be. I have begun to look at time differently in recent days. I believe that as we step into this new era of God's glory and God's soon-to-come Kingdom, there will be a supernatural acceleration and expansion of time for those who are fully serving God. God can supernaturally extend your time. God can bend your time. God can lengthen your days. Besides all of that, we literally have an eternity of time!

In the glory realms, when the powers of the age to come begin to manifest, time as we know it will be changed. The Lord will begin to expand and compress time for His friends! People ask me occasionally how I have written so many books so fast. Answer? God gives me supernatural grace and favor with time. I decree that time is my servant and according to my new friend, Joshua Mills, "God created time as a blessing to mankind. Time is not a curse to me, but time is my servant."[1]

Things that normally would take four hours to accomplish will be done in one hour. We will learn to live in the glory realms and understand that as the powers of the age to come are accelerating we can be given a supernatural extension of our natural days. We can live to be 120 or even older (though some of my friends think this kind of supernatural longevity may be unwise). We can be like Noah and live to be older and wiser than we currently expect or have faith for. That will enable us to be with Him longer on this side of eternity. Again, some of you reading this may not find this prospect for longer life attractive.

I just want more of Him; I want His presence, I want His fire, I want His glory, I want the Holy Spirit to be my best friend, I want the heavens to be opened up over my life. Sometimes you need the word. I love writing and reading the word of God; because as I write the scriptures down, it—the word—comes into my eye gates and matriculates back into my spirit. As I read God's anointed word, it becomes prophetic promises for me. It can also become a prophetic promise for you as you read this book too.

I want to look at the law of observation because it's an important avenue that can help you to step into the glory realms and activate you into the revelation of powers of the age to come. We are in a generation where God is raising up an end-time army that will walk in the powers of the age to come. That is why I have written this book. Are you interested in stepping into the powers of the age to come?

We want the anointing; we want the glory; we want the Holy Spirit. But there is something else; there is another level of Kingdom power that God's going to release to His friends at this hour. We can have it. It has to do with the law of observation. It has been said that what you feed your spirit on, what you focus on, what you observe is what you become. That's the law of observation (Genesis 30:31-43).

I'm believing this book will bring breakthroughs on many levels; more signs and wonders and more open heavens. Perhaps God will use it to help more people to open up to the supernatural in a greater way. I'm believing for signs and wonders to begin to break out in the charismatic churches and the mainline denominations as we step into this new season. I love them all. I was recently in Presbyterian churches in Korea. Those people are on fire for God; what a hunger, what a passion the Korean people have! It stirred my spirit so much to see people so hungry for God.

Love One Another

These different denominational people are all God's children, and I bless them. What I do nearly every Saturday night or Sunday morning is get into my prayer closet and begin to intercede and decree revival for my home church in Lee's Summit, Missouri, and for all the churches in my area and elsewhere. I pray for God to pour out His Spirit and anoint my pastor, Alan Koch, and for all the pastors and my brothers and sisters in Christ. I pray that the pastors will have visitations. I pray that the Kingdom of God would come with unprecedented power and unprecedented signs and wonders. I pray that the glory would fall in the Baptist churches and in the Catholic churches and in just every mainline denominational meeting.

Why am I telling you this? This is a key to open up the glory and to release the power of the Kingdom of God into your life.

Jesus said, "*A new commandment I give to you, that you love one another; as I have loved you, that you also love one another*" (John 13:34). Do you know why we sometimes don't get a breakthrough in our lives and in our ministries? It's because we are opinionated and many of us have unrighteous judgments in our hearts against our brothers and sisters in the Body of Christ. Better watch out! You need to love your brothers. Without God's love being spread abroad in our hearts, we become tethered to the temporal, carnal, or earthly realm. A judgmental and critical spirit will keep you from breaking into the heavenly places.

We can no longer afford to allow division and discord to abide in our hearts. Why? Because it's not the time you think it is and you are not where you think you are. We are here but we are somewhere else. And it's actually not the time you think it is because later the time is going to reverse; it's not the space-time continuum, it's not these angels of creative miracles and glory. It is that God has spoken from His throne of mercy and grace. We have crossed a chronological line on God's preordained calendar. The coming of the King is close at hand, and as God is beginning to release the powers of the age to come into the earthly or temporal realms, this affects time as we humans perceive it; though our understanding of time is elementary.

As this acceleration of the powers of the age to come increases, there will be a quickening of the Kingdom of Heaven. Time and space will be transformed. That is why it is not the time you think it is and you are not where you think you are. I believe that time as we know it has shifted in the spiritual dimensions. This shifting of time has begun to affect the events that are transpiring upon the earth. There is what I believe to be a rending or tearing of the space and time continuum that is occurring as the Father is speaking from His throne in the heavenly realms. That is why the law of observation is so important. There is a supernatural acceleration and manifestation of the things that we discern and observe in the glory realms at this hour.

God's Supernatural Calendar

All of this is for God's glory and to help accelerate the unfolding plans of the Lord to return. We have stepped into a God-ordained moment of history, and the dynamics of our world are changing in supernatural ways. Time and space as we know them will be forever transformed, in a moment and in the twinkling of an eye (1 Corinthians 15:52)! The Kingdom of God and the powers of the age to come will arrive unexpectedly. This shifting and expansion of time is one of the hidden mysteries of the powers of the age to come.

Hibernating Promises

I want to share some revelation and keys to help you develop a lifestyle of hosting the glory. These are keys to living a lifestyle of glory and are related to the law of observation and the unfolding plans and time of God's supernatural calendar. Let's start with Romans 4:17. Paul is speaking of Abraham who, though his body was as good as dead, God said Abram would be the father of many nations (vv. 18-19). In verse 17 Paul said, *"(as it is written, 'I have made you a father of many nations')* in

161

the presence of Him whom he believed—God." Some of you have prophetic words and promises from God. Perhaps they seem to be dead. They're not dead; they are only hibernating.

It's not the time you think it is. It is not the time to give up on the manifestation of your God-ordained destiny. When the scripture says, *"In the presence of Him,"* it is talking about the glory of God. My friend David Herzog teaches that glory plus declaration equals manifestation of miracles. Glory plus declaration equals acceleration into your God-ordained destiny. When it says, *"God, who gives life to the dead and calls those things which do not exist as though they did"* (v. 3), this describes speaking into the glory. When we decree into the glory, declaration plus glory equals manifestation of miracles. That's why we are seeing signs and wonders today.

This is for you. It's not just for me. You can walk in these miraculous aspects of the Kingdom of Heaven in your daily life. "Well, Kevin, I don't need the glory. I just go to church and I pay my tithes and I work my job and I pay my insurance and I've got my car and I don't need the glory and the power of God. I'm pretty satisfied with life." Yes, you need the revelation of the glory! You need the power of God in your life! When it starts to get dark, really dark, like we see in Isaiah 60:1-2 where it says rise and shine—we praise God for that—but it also says, *"Darkness shall cover the earth, and gross darkness the people"* (KJV), you will wish that you had the glory! When this shaking accelerates you will wish that you had the power! When this gross darkness comes, you are going to need the glory of God: *"But the LORD will arise over you, And His glory will be seen upon you"* (v. 2). There is a significant correlation between the glory realms and the powers of the age to come. That is why we are briefly looking at cultivating the glory realms in this book.

When there is no bread on the shelf in the grocery store, wouldn't it be nice to have angels of creative miracles to work sovereignty for you and then "poof" bread appears. The angels of God can provide for you and your family just like they did for the children of Israel (Psalm 103:20; 78:25; Numbers 11:31; Exodus 16:15). Even in January 2014 there was a hazardous chemical spill of 7,000 gallons of 4-methylcyclohexane methanol into the water supply near Charleston, West Virginia. The result was that about 300,000 people could not use their water.[2] We will begin to see more and more instances like this when food and water will not be readily available. Praise God for famine and droughts (1 Thessalonians 5:16-18). These indicate that Christ's return is close at hand.

I'm already putting my order in. I don't want just the white bread; I want honey wheat bread, the good stuff. I want the bread of heaven. I want the crystal clear water that comes from the throne of God and from the throne of the Lamb (Revelation 22). Remember the story in the Book of Exodus about the manna? *"When the children of Israel saw it, they said to one another, 'What is it?' For they did not know what it was. And Moses said to them, 'This is the bread which the LORD has given you to eat.'"* Why not? God gives life to the dead and calls those things which do not exist as though they do (Romans 4:17). We need to understand the law of observation and become equipped to operate in it in the coming days.

This will be a characteristic of the mature sons and daughters of the Most High God. They will call things into existence by the power of God and the words of their mouths. The Spirit and the power of *Ruach Ha Chodesh* will rest upon their breath. They will call those things that do not exist in this realm into existence (Romans 4:17). In the next chapter we will look at the correlation of the law of observation and the glory realms. Even your thoughts can become vehicles to manifest the powers of the age to come and the Kingdom of Heaven in your sphere of influence!

CHAPTER 17

As a Man Thinks—the Power That Works Within Us

Proverbs 23:7 tells us: *"For as he thinks in his heart, so is he."* Your thoughts are powerful. In fact, as the powers of the age to come increase, your thoughts will become more powerful than you might imagine. After all, God has promised that He would do above all that we could think ask or imagine according to *the power* that works in us (Ephesians 3:20)! So the question becomes, how much power of God is working within you?

You see, when you begin to live a lifestyle of glory, you can expect creative miracles and supernatural provision. These are all aspects of the powers of the age to come. It's getting a little unsettling for me now. Not that I'm at any great level of the glory, or this kind of power, but sometimes I can merely think about something and it just happens! I recently thought that I would like a new Swiss watch, and the same day a nice Swiss watch with a leather band arrived in the mail. Remember how the Lord supplied the prophet with water (1 Kings 19:6)? God can still do these same kinds of creative miracles today; these are attributes of the power of the age to come. These are characteristics of learning to dwell and live in the glory realms. This kind of supernatural lifestyle is possible for you when you become a friend of God, or a mature son or daughter of God. This is Kingdom life; and there is a strong correlation between the glory, the power, and the law of observation.

Fleas on a Hot Ash Pile

I can give you a perfect example of this dynamic. Kathy and I were about to eat at this magnificent buffet in Pusan, South Korea. We were the guests of a large group of pastors and leaders who had hosted several meetings. We were having dinner with all of these pastors and dignitaries. These Korean pastors are really precious people who love the Lord. You know, there's kind of tradition there in Korea—where you sit, who's got the honorable seat, and all that stuff. I'm just a country boy, and a country boy can survive; but, man, I just don't really care about traditions and seating protocol. I love people, but I don't really care where you want me to sit. You know what I mean? Let's just sit down and eat, for heaven's sake!

Jesus spoke about this kind of thing in Luke 14:8-10:

When you are invited by anyone to a wedding feast, do not sit down in the best place, lest one more honorable than you be invited by him; and he who invited you and him come and say to you, "Give place to this man," and then you begin with shame to take the lowest place. But when you are invited, go and sit down in the lowest place, so that when he who invited you comes he may say to you, "Friend, go up higher." Then you will have glory in the presence of those who sit at the table with you.

Hey, I just want to enjoy the Korean Kobe barbeque. Let's stop being concerned where everyone is supposed to sit and let's just enjoy our meal! I was not interested in having glory or recognition in the presence of those who sat at the table with me.

So we are moving around the table like fleas on a hot ash pile seeking to find the correct order of the seating arrangement. "You sit here." "No, you sit there by Pastor Ahaa." There was this young man waiting for all of us to stop hopping around. And I discerned by the Spirit that he was totally lost and a bit put off by Christians like our group (no offense intended here). He was greatly troubled; and I could discern that he was struggling with sin issues, but I knew that at one time he had walked close with God. I later discovered that this young man was a pastor's kid, a "PK." So everybody is talking about these things and they are all important things about the seating order and so on, but my heart is drawn to this young man. Do you know what his name was? His name was Gospel; that's the truth! Gospel was in pain; the Lord gave me a word of knowledge to share with him. So I quietly snuck off to the buffet, and I kind of cornered him and said, "Hey, is your back hurting?"

He said, "How did you know about my back problem?"

I said, "I just know things sometimes. Here, let me pray for you." So I prayed for him; and, *instantly*, his back gets healed. I said, "You know what? The Lord wants me to tell you something. I believe that God wants you to know that the door is still open for you."

He went, "Ooooooh," and he started weeping. It was so simple. He was the one waiting on our table. So the pastors, Kathy and I, along with everyone else in our group, are busy eating. We are munching down on kimchi, which I love, and other great Korean food, like raw octopus; and most of them can't see what's going on. We don't see the tears in his eyes. We don't discern the pain in Gospel's heart. They are not discerning the issue. This young man, Gospel, is waiting on us; and we don't even notice him because we are busy doing our own stuff. So, later I went to get some dessert, and he comes up to me and grabs me by the sleeve. He starts weeping again and said, "How did you know all that stuff? My back feels better!"

Here is the point, in reference to the powers of the age to come and the power of your thoughts. I said, "You know, brother; God loves you"; and the Lord began to give me some more revelation for him. His English was good but it wasn't perfect, so in my mind I just thought, "I wish Debra was here," because she was the interpreter working with me. So at that very instant, I turned around because someone is tapping me on the shoulder; it's Debra. She helped me to minister to Gospel more fully.

So, you see, when you live a lifestyle of glory, these things happen time and time again. You can just think about something and it manifests! That's what you need. It's not just for the evangelist, it's not just for the apostle; it's for everybody. I mean for everybody! Perhaps your family is not serving God the way they should? You don't necessarily need to preach to them and quote the scriptures to them; get in the glory and ask God to give you His divine revelation. So when you learn to live in the glory, you can begin to walk in greater levels of the power of God. Again, this is an aspect of the powers of the age to come. You can just think about something, and it manifests!

The Great Cloud of Witnesses Are Elated

I am going to give you a few keys to the glory realms that will help you to access the powers of the age to come. Do you understand that the Scripture really is alive? It really is living. Let's go to Hebrews 12:22-23: "*You have come to Mount Zion and to the city of the living God, the heavenly Jerusalem, to an innumerable company of angels, to the general assembly and church of the firstborn who are registered in heaven, to God the Judge of all, to the spirits of just men made perfect.*" Wait a minute; who is this passage referring to? Who is the author of Hebrews talking about here? Who are the spirits of just men made perfect? He's talking about the great cloud of witnesses (v. 1). He's talking about those who have preceded us into heaven. This scripture is referring to our heavenly family.

In Ephesians 3:14-15 Paul says, "*I bow my knees to the Father of our Lord Jesus Christ, from whom the whole family in heaven and earth is named.*" You see, we have a family in heaven. I've seen the great cloud of witnesses peering down over the golden railing of heaven at what's going on in meetings and in church services. Those of the great cloud of witnesses are actually very interested in what's going on in our lives. They are excited about the day and the hour that we live in. I believe that those of the great cloud of witnesses are elated because they know that the Lord is raising up mature sons and daughters of the

Most High God. As we learned earlier in this book, sometimes they crash our parties!

They're excited that people are getting the revelation that we can co-labor with heaven. They are excited that God is about to release the powers of the age to come to His friends on the earth. Again, I call these friends of God the royal priesthood according to the order of Melchizedek. That's absolutely biblical. They are mature sons and daughters of God who walk in holiness and sanctification. They will live a lifestyle of peace and purity and walk in unity and harmony with the Spirit of God. All of these things are keys to hosting the glory of God and learning to recognize and discern the powers of the age to come.

Hebrews 12:24 goes on to tell us we have also come "*to Jesus the Mediator of the new covenant, and to the blood of sprinkling that speaks better things than that of Abel.*" This speaks about the tabernacle where the Aaronic priests sprinkled the offerings and sprinkled the utensils there. You see, there is a tabernacle in the heavenly realms. We can enter into the glory realms; we can enter into the tabernacle not made with hands; we can enter into the holy of holies. This is the tabernacle in heaven to which Jesus Christ gave us the key by the shedding and sprinkling of His blood. Revelation 1:5-6 says the blood of Jesus cleanses us; it makes us righteous and holy that we might be kings and priests to our God and Father.

We know that God the Father is seated in heavenly realms. Recently in prayer I literally went to the throne and the Father reached out and pulled me into the glory. As I shared earlier in the chapter about the Father's throne. It's been happening more and more. How would you like the Father to just reach out and pull you into the glory? It can happen; just learn to speak to Papa God as a man speaks to a friend. Some people are afraid of supernatural experiences like this because the Bible says if you see God you will die (Exodus 33:20).

He Spoke on Earth

If you believe that, that's probably what will happen to you. You could die! That would be great! My Bible also says God, through the finished work of Jesus Christ—through His shed blood, His death upon a Cross, His burial in an unused grave, and His resurrection—has made me a king and priest to minister unto my God and Father. Now, how am I going to minister to God the Father unless I come into His presence? It's all part of your life as a royal priest according to the order of Melchizedek. Really all that means is being transformed more fully into the image of Jesus and learning to co-labor with the powers of the age to come! It is easy! This is the fulfillment of Ephesians 4:13: *"Till we all come to the unity of the faith and of the knowledge of the Son of God, to a perfect man, to the measure of the stature of the fullness of Christ."*

Look at Hebrews 12:25: *"See that you do not refuse Him who speaks."* What "Him" is this passage referring to? The Father! *"For if they did not escape who refused Him who spoke on earth."* Remember when God called the whole nation of Israel to the mountain and He spoke and the whole earth trembled and shook (Exodus 19). The Israelites said, "This is too freaky! Moses, you go up and talk to Him for us because if we see Him or hear Him we'll die!" (20:19). They put a curse on themselves.

Some of us are still living under that curse and we don't realize it. Unknowingly our mind set is that if we actually see Him or if we actually hear God speaking to us we will die.

If this statement is true for you, then it is possible that you have become trapped in an ungodly dimension that is empowering a curse in your life and family. That kind of ungodly mindset is a curse. It is a stronghold. Many of us have Jewish DNA; and we are definitely grafted into the tree of Christ. So as Christians we serve a Jewish God. Some of us have that curse from Exodus 20:19 operating in our lives unless we realize it, discern it, and overcome such a curse by the blood of the Lamb. God was seeking to speak to all of the people of Israel, and He still wants to speak to all of the Hebrew people today. In fact, He wants to speak to you as a man speaks to a friend (Exodus 33:11).

Let's look at this dynamic further in Hebrews 12:25-26: "*If they did not escape who refused Him who spoke on earth, much more shall we not escape if we turn away from Him who speaks from heaven, whose voice then shook the earth; but now He has promised, saying, 'Yet once more I shake not only the earth, but also heaven.'*" Let me just repeat this again, that's the hour that we live in. God is speaking from His throne of righteousness and mercy but it's also a throne of justice.

And I believe that this nation that I live in (America) is at a hinge of history, as some prophetic people say. I believe that God is speaking and He is going to shake this nation. *He IS shaking this nation!* We've already seen it; this shaking is going to continue. God will continue to shake the whole earth! That's another reason why we need to live in His presence, why we need to live in His glory. We need to be able to come boldly before the throne of grace that we might find mercy in our time of need (Hebrews 4:16). God is speaking and the earth is shaking. But with this shaking is coming the release of the powers of the age to come. We just need to *learn to discern* it! We just need to embrace the powers of the age to come. In the gross darkness, God's glory and light will shine the brightest. God will use the darkness for His purposes and draw the lost to Him and into the Kingdom of His Son.

Hebrews 12:27 tells us: "*Now this, 'Yet once more,' indicates the removal of those things that are being shaken, as of things that are made, that the things which cannot be shaken may remain.*" Do you feel some shaking in your life right now? Everyone is feeling shaking at this hour. If you're not, praise God! You're walking in a very high level of righteousness, holiness, and friendship with God. But God is shaking the entire earth and the nation of America. He will continue to shake this nation. In fact, *He is shaking ALL nations* at this hour. And everything that you have in your life that's not founded on the Rock, Jesus, He will shake; and it may fall. That's why we need the glory. That's why we need a close, personal relationship with God. That's why we need to be able to enter into His presence and learn to be transformed into overcomers (Revelation 3:21; 21:7). That is an important reason why we need to understand how to access the powers of the age to come.

In Hebrews 12:28 the author tells us, "*Therefore, since we are receiving a kingdom which cannot be shaken, let us have grace.*" Sometimes when I have been granted heavenly grace and I have entered into the heavenly throne room, the Lord will release angels of grace. We need to receive those angels of grace. If you don't believe that, then it's probably not going to work for you. I need all of the grace I can get. I have seen the Father release angels of grace and mercy into the earthly realms.

I have experienced immediate manifestations of grace and favor in situations as a result of supernatural experiences like this one. A critical dynamic of the powers of the age to come is the ability to discern and recognize God's angelic beings whom God has empowered to release blessings and ministry into our lives and into the lives of those we are called to minister to. This is a dynamic of the law of observation. When we learn to discern and observe heavenly things (in the heavenly dimensions) these same heavenly things manifest upon the earth in our lives, like grace for example.

The Fire of God

Again, these are dynamics of the powers of the age to come. I need all the mercy I can get. Why do we need things like I am describing? So that *"we may serve God acceptably with reverence and godly fear. For our God is a consuming fire"* (Hebrews 12:28-29). God is burning things out of our lives that keep us from Him. That fire is His mercy. When we submit to God's cleansing and healing fire, we are being prepared to step into the powers of the age to come. We are being prepared to be totally transformed into the very image and character of Christ! I get excited about these things, and you should be too! These shakings and judgments are God's mercy.

So I've got a key that can help you live a lifestyle of glory: submit to God and allow the fire of God to burn from you anything that keeps you from walking in holiness, anything that keeps you from walking in intimacy with the Holy Spirit, anything that keeps you from God. Give any hindrances to Him! It's much easier that way. Learn to allow the fire of God to burn it out of you, for our God is a consuming fire. That's why we need the glory and the revelation of the Law of Observation. In the day and the hour that we are living in, these aspects of the Kingdom of Heaven are critical.

In the next chapter we will begin to look at the powers of the age to come in more detail as I share several miraculous testimonies that helped to cement my understanding of the power of the Trinity.

CHAPTER 18

The Powers of the Age to Come

Is there anything upon the earth is not found in the Scriptures? I believe that the answer is no. I believe that the word of God will stand when the world falls. The word of God is all encompassing and in the Scriptures the Lord has concealed many hidden and mysterious treasures. Over the last decade the Lord has taken me on a miraculous journey. When I received Jesus Christ as my Lord and Savior, I opened a spiritual door that allowed the God of the universe to transform my life. The Lord initiated a metamorphosis that took me from poverty to prosperity; from sickness to health; from hopelessness to hope.

The Lord rescued me from the kingdom of darkness and translated me into His Kingdom of Love and Light. If you have read the books that I have previously penned, you will know that God has truly worked a miracle in my life and has genuinely transformed me into a new creation (2 Corinthians 5:17). You may wish to consider that God can initiate the same kind of supernatural transformation in your life too. Along the way the Lord has been very patient with me and has shown me different aspects and truths of His Kingdom in small increments and portions that I could understand and receive at each step and stage of my journey.

For whatever reason, I suppose that it is only the grace of God, the Lord began to minister to me through angelic ministry. The Lord initiated a transformation in my life in February 2001 when I was born again for the third or fourth time (I apologize if the concept of losing one's salvation does not conform to some of your theology). In November of that year, the Lord accelerated the manifestation of His Kingdom in my life when the heavens opened over my life in Springdale, Newfoundland, Canada. You could say that I witnessed a spiritual gate or portal of glory appear. This was yet again another mystery that I have pondered in my heart for years! On that night, November 25, 2001, I began to see into the spiritual realm with great clarity and consistency. The Lord opened my spiritual eyes, and I saw the Lord Jesus descend into a small church, Living Waters Ministries. During that time the Lord came over and stood over me and spoke to me as a man would speak to a friend, commissioning me into the ministry.

One aspect of these incredible encounters with the Kingdom of God and its King was the ongoing ability to see and discern God's angels. (These supernatural events are well documented in my two trilogies of books on God's angels and on the seer anointing if you care to learn more about God's angelic beings and the seer anointing.) At any rate, I became aware that the Lord was employing angelic ministry to help spark this God-ordained metamorphosis or transformation in my life. This also initiated an extended season in which I was given the grace to ascend into the heavenly realms and to fellowship with Jesus in the heavenly places (Ephesians 1:3). This supernatural process has unfolded over the last decade line upon line and precept upon precept (Isaiah 28:10, 13), and the Lord has given me more and more revelation concerning the hidden mysteries of His Kingdom and how the Kingdom of Heaven affects the earthly realms.

Kingdom Authority

The Lord began to teach me from His word in a supernatural fashion, for which I am eternally grateful and give unto Him all of the glory. The Lord began to show me the various levels of His power and His Kingdom. You see, the Lord will give you more responsibility and revelation line upon line and precept upon precept. As we are obedient to do those things the Lord shows us, He releases greater levels of Kingdom authority to us. I call this our sphere of influence. We all have a sphere of influence that the Lord entrusts to each of us. Let me encourage you with the fact that radical obedience is the key to expanding your sphere of influence and the level of Kingdom power that you are entrusted with. There is no shortcut here.

As this process began to unfold in my life, the Lord began to teach me about the power of His word, the Canon of Scripture. The Holy Spirit taught me that I could depend upon His word, and as time passed I grew to trust that I could use God's word as I prayed. I could remind Father God of the promises that He had given me in His word (Isaiah 43:26). For example, we find that we can increase our faith by reading and studying God's anointed word (Romans 10:17). I also discovered that as we are diligent to believe God's word, we are privileged to develop our faith; and as we are diligent to exercise our faith, God will reward us with spiritual gifts (Hebrews 11:6).

Later the Lord began to give me more understanding that there is supernatural healing that comes from His word (Psalm 107:20). As I was diligent to believe God for these promises from His Kingdom, He began to reveal other hidden and mysterious secrets of His Kingdom to me in the area of healing and miracles. I believe that for some of you reading this right now God will give you the desires of your heart and launch you into these same kinds of supernatural experiences. The Creator of heaven and earth will begin to release to you the hidden mysteries and secrets of the Kingdom of Heaven.

The Anointing of the Holy Spirit

So I saw that the Lord took me from the principles in His word concerning faith and healing to another level of spiritual authority in His Kingdom. This was the realm of the gifts of the Holy Spirit, or the anointing of the Holy Spirit (1 Corinthians 12). Through the visitations of the Lord that I had mentioned earlier and through the ministry and help of others more mature in the matters of the Kingdom than myself, I began to grow and learn about the dynamics of the anointing of the Holy Spirit and began to minister in the power and gifts of the Holy Spirit.

I praise God for the ministry of the Holy Spirit, the presence of the Holy Spirit, and the communion of the Holy Spirit every day! *"Thank You for the Holy Spirit, Lord!"* By this time and through radical obedience, the Lord had supernaturally launched me out into international ministry. By the grace of

God, Kathy and I have traveled to over thirty-eight nations ministering in the power of the Holy Spirit and in the gifts of the Spirit. This level of Kingdom power is called "the anointing" by many people.

We have seen God work a lot of miracles, signs, and wonders around the earth. We have seen the deaf hear, the blind see, and paralytics walk. In Tanzania we witnessed the dead raised by the awesome power and grace of Almighty God on February 26, 2006. However, the greatest miracle that we witnessed has been the tens of thousands of precious people in many nations who have prayed to receive Jesus Christ as Lord and Savior.

Salvation is the greatest miracle of all. (If you would like to pray to receive the Lord Jesus Christ, you can turn to the prayer at the end of this book and be saved or born again right now.) Still, in the midst of the years of traveling, I knew deep down that there was more. There was another level of the power of God that we had not touched yet. For example, on the Sunday night when the little girl was raised from the dead no one had touched her. It was a sovereign miracle. That night I discerned there was an unusually high level of the power of God present. I believe that power was responsible for the little girl arising from the dead (Luke 5:17). Perhaps this was the power of the Father? I called this kind of power "resurrection power." What was the key to discerning this heavenly power? When and how does it come or manifest?

That miracle had nothing to do with the word, or faith, or angelic ministry. It was no man's anointing or gift through which God released His resurrection power to raise the dead. It was the Father's sovereignty and Kingdom power that was present to raise the dead that day. The Lord also used this expe-rience to teach me something about His Kingdom. The lesson I learned? God does not need me to work miracles! He does not need my faith. He does not need my anointing. He does not need my preaching or gifting at all. I fasted (periodically) and prayed about this from 2006 to up to this present time. There was something missing. Surely there was a hidden mystery in all of this, and I purposed in my heart to search this heavenly secret out (Proverbs 25:2). What was this hidden power?

Most of what I had understood and heard taught in the pew were messages about the anointing of the Holy Spirit alone. I also knew that at times that God released angels of healing to co-labor with us, but I always sensed that there was more. There is surely a hidden mystery surrounding God's heart to release His miracles and His resurrection power. So I searched the word and asked the Lord for more revelation. After some time we began to experience hundreds more miracles and healings happening in what I call the sovereign realm. In other words, no one laid hands upon the people to release their mir-acles and healings. We began to see a lot of tumors dissolve and deaf ears open in this way, through the sovereign realm of healing and miracle ministry.

More Kingdom Power

During this time we began to experience a higher level of King-dom power than when ministering with the anointing of the Holy Spirit alone. Over time God began to move more and more frequently in greater levels of His power and grace to release miracles, signs, and wonders in our meetings sovereignly. I do not believe that it was an anointing of the Holy Spirit alone that released the miracles, signs, and wonders in our meetings. I do not believe that it was an anointing of the Holy Spirit alone that raised the little girl from the dead. No. That was a level of resurrection power that, in my estimation, was considerably above and beyond the anointing that I was blessed to experience on February 26, 2006, in Tanzania.

At this point in time we were not laying hands upon people to heal them (although we certainly believe in the biblical doctrine of the laying on of hands to heal). We were traveling the Lakes District of Tanzania and conducting Miracle Outreaches. By the grace of God we saw over 19,000 receive Jesus as Lord and Savior in those seven weeks. However, we also witnessed literally hundreds of miracles at the altar. Blind eyes were healed, deaf ears opened, tumors dissolved, paralytics walked, and all manner of sickness was healed. I never touched any of the people who testified to these miracles. They were all healed by the power of God.

I was very grateful to the Lord for this kind of sovereign healing because it did not empower the worship of man in God's people. Instead it forced the people to look to God alone. As a result we experienced a lot of salvations. That was an answer to prayer. We must focus our worship on God alone. We must never allow the man or the gifts of God resident upon a man or woman replace the Messiah. This is a form of idol worship, and God hates idol worship. This manifestation of these kinds of sovereign miracles and healing has only increased since February 2006. To God be the glory, honor, and praise!

At times when the sovereign realm of God's power would manifest, there would be a powerful presence of the Lord hovering around the meeting. Ah, the glory of God! So we began to learn to move from the anointing into the glory realms or sovereign realms of the miraculous. We began to discern that the glory realm was different than the realm of the anointing of the Holy Spirit. The glory of God seemed to multiply the power and level of the anointing of the Holy Spirit. Therefore, I determined that we need both the glory of God and the anointing of the Holy Spirit to operate in tandem to complement and augment one another.

I believe that God wants you to do the same. We soon began to learn that in the glory creative miracles are possible. Later, we learned that when you minister in the anointing of the Holy Spirit in the glory, even greater miracles, signs, and wonders manifest to confirm the preaching of the word of God. So as we experimented and implemented this new understanding, we began to see even more signs and wonders. The miracles and healings seemed to come easier when we learned to host the glory of God. Yet, somehow I understood that there is even more power of the Kingdom that is available at this hour. So I continued to seek the Lord's heart in this matter.

Love and Unity

I believe that we have stepped into a new dispensation of grace. The Lord is releasing a greater level of the power of God into the earth at this hour. Please allow me to state an important fact for the purists and the Pentecostals reading this. God will never replace the anointing or the gifts of the Holy Spirit.

We need the Holy Spirit. But I believe that the Father has pre-ordained for the power of the Trinity to be poured out in these last days. There are two keys that can accelerate this dynamic or the release of the power of the Trinity, in my opinion. We will see the release of the greater anointings and the greater activation of the power of heaven released or manifested when God's people begin to truly walk in God's love and in true unity.

When ministries and individuals (who are anointed by God) come together in love and unity, there is a supernatural dynamic that is released from the heavenly realms. There is a commanded blessing that the Father releases (Psalm 133). When we put our individual agendas on hold and work in harmony to bring forth God's agenda and build His Kingdom the oil of heaven is poured out upon us in the earthly realm (Hebrews 1:9; Psalm 133). As we have learned to minister in love and unity with other ministers who carry the legitimate heart of God and the true anointing of the Holy Spirit, there is a multiplication of the power and glory of God that is released. This is again another key that can help to open the gates of heaven over your life. This can empower you and your sphere of influence. Understanding and implementing this simple principle can help you to experience the greater works that Jesus Christ has commanded for you to manifest in your life and ministry (John 14:12). This has been labeled the "cooper-ate anointing."

Really this dynamic is a culmination or comingling of the rivers of God and a convergence of what I refer to as the sevenfold flow of the rivers or seven anointings of the Spirit. In Genesis 26:32-33 we see that Isaac found pure water at the seventh well that was dug: *"It came to pass the same day that Isaac's servants came and told him about the well which they had dug, and said to him, 'We have found water.' So he called it Shebah."* The number seven represents completion or perfection. Shebah was the well of seven flows or seven rivers of pure water. Picture it as seven separate artesian springs of pure power bubbling up from your belly (John 7:38). The Lord has spoken to me about this Kingdom principle. When there is purity and an artesian flow of the fullness of the seven rivers or anointings of God, there will be an unprecedented outpouring of the glory and power of God. I believe that this will be an outpouring of the powers of the age to come. This outpouring will help usher in the great last days' harvest of the Kingdom of Heaven and help prepare us for the return of the Messiah. That is called true revival!

Here are some of the pure rivers of Heaven that the Lord has poured out upon the earth up to this hour: the word of God or the Canon of Scripture, the faith realm, the anointing of the Holy Spirit, the power of the Holy Spirit, the glory realm, the seer realm, or the release of angelic ministry. It is possible that the seventh river of God will be the powers of the age to come. Unlike many other theologians, I do not necessarily believe that the powers of the age to come will be limited to millennial reign of Christ. Nor will the powers of the age to come be totally tied to the return of Christ. I believe that the Lord will begin to release this kind of Kingdom power and Kingdom authority through His friends at this hour. Again, I believe that it is in the Creator's plans to employ the creature to help to reestablish His Kingdom upon the earth. God will raise up forerunners who will prepare the way of the Lord (Malachi 3:1; Isaiah 40:3; Luke 3:4).

One of the ways that the Lord is beginning to accomplish this is by raising up a royal priesthood according to the order of Melchizedek. These people will not fit the mold that most of the church is looking for or expecting. God will begin to use the most unlikely and seemingly unfit people to release His Kingdom in the powers of the age to come. It will be the same in the days to come when the spiritual leaders of the day see the fullness of the power of Christ and the power of the Trinity released that they will marvel. Perhaps when the modern day leaders see the boldness of God's people, they will perceive that they are uneducated and untrained and they too will marvel. So they will realize that these anointed ones—these men, women, and children, these forerunners—have been with Jesus, in the heavenly realms (Acts 4:13).

I believe that the Lord is activating His people to operate in the "seer anointing" or the seer realm at this hour in a great and mighty way. Actually this is the gift of discerning of spirits that is being restored to the earth at this hour (1 Corinthians 12:10). God will begin to raise up and anoint the eyes and ears of many of His friends to see and hear well from heaven or the other spiritual dimensions. At times they will begin to discern the Lord's angelic hosts, His angels, and occasionally the great cloud of witnesses (Hebrews 12:1). Please remember that God is not the God of the dead but the living (Matthew 22:32). So I want to make this point perfectly clear: I am not referring to necromancy or communing with the dead.

Actually, Jesus had a supernatural encounter where He spoke to members of the great cloud of witnesses. That incident is well documented in Matthew 17:1-3: *"Now after six days Jesus took Peter, James, and John his brother, led them up on a high mountain by themselves; and He was transfigured before them. His face shone like the sun, and His clothes became as white as the light. And behold, Moses and Elijah appeared to them, talking with Him."* So as Jesus spoke to Moses and Elijah was He practicing necromancy?

The answer is absolutely not. The Lord experienced a supernatural encounter where two members of the great cloud of witnesses appeared to Him to give Him council and wisdom. I believe that many ordinary people will begin to have similar encounters where they will discern that members of the great cloud of witnesses will be present. At other times they will discern angelic activity as well. Really what we are speaking about is God raising up mature sons and daughters of God, who will be recreated in the very image of Jesus and who will learn to grow in Kingdom authority. These royal priests according to the order of Melchizedek will learn to do the greater works just as the Messiah did. They will recreate Christ in their spheres of influence and will at times be given the grace and anointing by God to live and minister in the power of the age to come. They will walk in the seer anointing.

This supernatural anointing or power will be delegated from the Father and the Holy Spirit to His friends. It will be a release of the pure seven rivers of God to the earth through the Lord's anointed ones. Men, women, and children two to a hundred and two years old will be graced to minister in this type of heavenly power and authority. And there shall be nothing impossible for them. Many will heal the sick, cleanse the lepers, raise the dead, and cast out demons by the power of God. They will freely release and impart the gifts and anointings of the Holy Spirit and the Kingdom to the world as the Lord leads them (Matthew 10:7-8; Romans 1:11). Again, I believe that this kind of Kingdom power and anointing is for everyone and not reserved for "chosen vessels." It will be a whosoever anointing.

Before I move on to the conclusion of this book, I sense that the Holy Spirit would have me to share a powerful testimony about a few days that changed an entire city in 2006. The powers of the age to come visited us in the village of Beucelecelli, Tanzania, and the result was incredible.

CHAPTER 19

The Reverential Power and Awe of God Witnessed in Tanzania

In February of 2006 I traveled to a small city in the bush of northwest Tanzania called Beucelecelli. At the time this region has a population of an estimated 40,000 with many others living in the surrounding area. Beucelecelli is fairly close to Rwanda. A local bishop had arranged this open-air, soul-winning outreach, and I was not aware of the extent that we would need to travel to reach our destination. The trip to Beucelecelli involved a two-hour boat ride, and then a long, bone-jarring, six-hour drive over grueling roads to reach the city. I was exhausted when we did make it to the town and decided to rest and pray.

The heavens were truly brass over my head, and it seemed that I could not get any breakthrough in prayer. It was extremely hot and humid and I was sweaty and dusty, and there was no running water in my hostel. In addition to this, I was feeling a considerable amount of opposition in the spirit. I felt the need for some fasting. The bishop came to my room in the evening and told me that the host pastors were requesting to meet with me for dinner. However, I declined their invitation, telling Isaya that I felt the need for fasting and prayer. I prayed nearly all night and still did not get any real breakthrough. When the sun came up the next morning, I did not have any clear direction for the ministry for the first night of the meetings; so I continued to fast and pray. About two in the afternoon, I finally heard from the Lord. The Holy Spirit told me this, "*I want you to stand up on the platform and tell the people that the God you serve, Jesus Christ, is real, He is alive; and Jesus says to tell you that we will see the rain fall on these crusade meetings before we leave your city.*"

I said, "*OK, Lord, but you know that people will not stand in the rain to hear the Gospel.*" So I was a little concerned with these unexpected directions. When the bishop came to get me to go to the meeting, I was glad to see about 4,000 people waiting on the meeting grounds. They were hungry to hear the Gospel. The first thing that I did was to stand up and declare with as much confidence as I could muster, "The God I serve, Jesus Christ of Nazareth, is real, He is alive; and Jesus says to tell you that we will see the rain fall on these crusade meetings before we leave your city." I was later told that I was the first "*mzungu mhubiri,*" or white preacher, to ever preach a healing outreach in the city. The Lord was faithful, and we saw several dozen miracles that night as we declared the Gospel of the Kingdom. There were also several hundred who responded to the altar call to be born again. They prayed to receive Jesus as their Savior and Lord. I had thought it to be a very good night. That is, until I met with the host pastors for dinner after the meeting.

Brave and Bold?

I went to my hostel and took a quick sink bath with one of my last bottles of Kilimanjaro water, and then I went to meet the pastors. The very first thing that the main pastor said through the interpretation of the bishop was, "You are a very brave and bold man!" That caught me off guard; and I said, "I am?" "Yes," he said, "you have stood on the platform in the full view of the whole pubic and everyone and you have promised the people that it will rain on my city. It has not rained here for eleven months and we are in severe famine." When my new friend told me this, I suddenly lost my appetite and quietly decided that I would eat little of the proffered "skinny chicken" and that I would continue to give myself to much more prayer and fasting. Later, when the bishop and I were alone, he told me that some of the pastors were concerned for my safety. It seemed they felt that some of the Muslims in the city might seek to stone me as a "false prophet" if it did not, in fact, rain within the next two days. This gave me reason to pause and press into the Kingdom of God all the more!

I returned to prayer in my small hostel and again found the heavens "brass" over my head. Sometimes it is just better to worship! I had brought my portable CD player and began to earnestly worship the Lord. I chose the Michael W. Smith song "Let it rain"! Yes, that was exactly what I needed. I needed the floodgates of heaven to open up and for God to pour out not only rain in the natural, but also His presence and power in the Spirit. I prayed and worshiped all night. When the sun came up the sky was as clear as a bell and the bright hot African sun pierced the flimsy blue curtains of my hostel room. I went to God In prayer again.

"Lord, You told me yesterday to tell these people that it was going to rain on this city. Lord, do You know that it has not rained here for eleven months?" (Of course, He knew.) I struggled in prayer all day. I was concerned and was asking for a miracle in the form of rain. During this time the Michael W. Smith song, "Let it rain," was repeating on my portable CD player and my mini speakers! About 1 p.m. I began to hear a sound... thud, thud, thud. Suddenly the sound multiplied! Huge rain drops started falling on the metal roof of my hostel... thud, thud, thud. Suddenly there was an earsplitting crack of thunder, and an instant bolt of lightning lit up the street in front of my room. A lightning bolt had hit home in the center of Beucelecelli, and the rain was falling in buckets. It was an instant deluge. Torrential rain began to fall from the cloudburst. I have never seen it rain so hard, with the one exception of the time I rode out a hurricane in the Virgin Islands. This downpour was what meteorologists might call a microburst.

I jumped to my feet to dance, but I could not hear the Michael W. Smith song, "Let it rain," because the rain was pounding so heavily upon the tin roof! I turned the volume on my little stereo up as loud as it would go, and began to dance and sing before the Lord with all of my heart! Let it rain! Let it rain! Open the flood gates of heaven! Glory to God in the highest! It was pouring rain; I had never seen anything like this in my life! It rained so hard that water actually began to stream in under the door of my hostel room. To my astonishment, I heard people laughing and dancing in the streets.

Presence and Great Power

When I looked out the window of the room, the people of Beucelecelli were dancing in the streets. They had buckets, pails, and any other containers that would collect the water; and were celebrating the deluge! I was starting to think that I knew how Noah must have felt. The atmosphere was electric, and you could sense that there had been a dramatic shift in the spiritual climate over the city and region. The heavens had opened over Beucelecelli (see Deuteronomy 28:12). I believe that God had released a signs and wonders or harvester angel who had stepped into the village of Beucelecelli at the instant that the lightning bolt struck. The earsplitting thunder and instantaneous lightning bolt were signs in the natural of the breaking open of the heavens in the spiritual realm. I could literally feel an unusually high level of God's presence and power hovering over the entire city. A spiritual window or gate had opened into the heavenly realms.

Somewhere around 3 p.m. I began to realize that if it kept raining like this the second night of the crusade might well be canceled. Again, I decided that it would be a good time to return to prayer and have some dialog with my Father. *"Lord,"* I began, *"You know if it keeps raining like this the people will not come to hear the Gospel, and if they do not come to hear the Gospel, then not many will be saved today."* I continued like this for some time. The heavy rain continued to fall relentlessly pounding the tin roof... thud, thud, thud. I knew that the bishop was busy keeping our equipment dry and making alternate plans, so I decided not to bother him with a call. The supernatural microburst continued unabated for another hour. By now, the crusade was one hour late getting started. About 4:30 p.m. the Lord spoke to me and said

> *The bishop will call you at 5:14. When he calls, he will tell you that he is on the way to get you. Be ready; I am going to do something special in this city today. I am going to reveal My glory and My power here. You will not have much time to preach, so when you stand on the platform, put on your sunglasses and tell the people this, "The God I serve, Jesus Christ of Nazareth, is real, He is alive; and Jesus says to tell you that the sun will shine on this crusade meeting today, and we will see mighty miracles of God."*

In my heart I thought, "Awesome!" In my mind I thought, "Boy, it sure is raining awfully hard!"

At exactly 5:14 my cell phone rang and it was the bishop telling me that he was on the way to get me. When I arrived at the soccer grounds where the meetings were being held, it was still raining heavily. I was astonished to see an estimated 4,000 people standing in the downpour waiting to hear the Gospel. I had been in dozens of crusade meetings up to then, and had never seen a crowd stand in the rain to hear the Gospel in Africa! When the bishop handed me the microphone I stepped up to the platform and, reaching into my pocket and putting on my sunglasses, told the people, "The God I serve, Jesus Christ of Nazareth, is real, He is alive; and Jesus says to tell you people that the sun will shine on this crusade meeting, and we will see mighty miracles of God today!"

Fractured Skies, Open Heavens, and Rainbows!

I began to preach and, within fifteen minutes, the dark overcast sky began to subside a little, although the rain was still falling very hard. There I was, with my sunglasses on, peering out through the rain drops. Within my heart I was praying for God to show up as I preached His word. The rain slowly let up by degrees. Five minutes later, one single, lone sunbeam instantaneously cracked the sky, and a brilliant stroke of sunshine fell upon the crusade grounds. The lone sunbeam cut through the darkness like a laser and illuminated only the soccer stadium and the crusade grounds. The microburst continued to pour out much-needed rain in the surrounding area.

I let out a sigh of relief, and to my astonishment, I could see a perfect circle in the clouds above. I could actually see the open heaven over the city. The supernatural sunbeam fell at about an 80 degree angle hitting the grounds. All around the rest of the area it was still dark and raining heavily. To my amazement, when the brilliantly bright sunbeam fractured the dark sky, people began to pour into the crusade grounds. Within five minutes, several thousand more people appeared out of nowhere and doubled the number of people who were on hand. A few minutes later, I was just about to give an altar call to receive Jesus Christ as Savior when Wade Holland broke my train of thought. Wade was tugging frantically, pulling on my wet white suit jacket sleeve. I turned to see what in the world it was about to find him pointing excitedly at the sky directly above the platform and the altar.

What a glorious sign and wonder the Lord had given the wonderful precious people of Beucelecelli. I turned to see the most magnificent double rainbow that I have ever witnessed. It was so close that I felt that I could reach out and break off a piece and taste it! Immediately the Holy Spirit took over the meeting. The power of God fell in an unusual way. I told the people of Beucelecelli that God had given them a sign in the heavens. I said that; "No white preacher can make it rain or make the sun shine; only God in heaven could do those things." I told the people about Noah, and how God gave Noah a covenant but that we had a better covenant in Christ Jesus! The atmosphere had broken open and the power of God was now present to heal (see Luke 5:17). Were we experiencing the power of the age to come?

The Power of God

I could feel the presence and power of God tangible hanging in the air. The hair on my left arm stood on end, and I knew that a healing angel was standing nearby. In fact, I was certain that an army of God's angelic hosts had invaded the city to minister along with me that evening. I never saw the healing angel or any other angels in Beucelecelli. However, I could sense their presence extremely strongly along with the accompanying power of God to heal that was released as the heavens opened. The power of God was soon to be witnessed by all those who were present on the grounds.

I told the people if they wanted to be born again and to have a covenant relationship with Jesus Christ the Son of the Living God, to respond by coming to the altar. An estimated

4,000 quickly came forward to pray to receive Jesus. After I led them in the prayer of salvation, I found these words coming out of my mouth, "The message and preaching of the Cross is foolishness to those who are perishing and going to burn for eternity in hell, but to those who are being saved, to those who are going to inherit eternal life in heaven and paradise, it is the power of God! The power of God is here to heal! We are going to see God do mighty miracles now!" It seemed as if the power of God multiplied to an extent that I had never experienced.

At that instant there was a crack of loud thunder, and then I heard a very loud and terrifying scream. The hair on the back of my neck stood on end. Suddenly hundreds of people began to scream! The power of God multiplied again, and immediately hundreds of people began to violently manifest demons. The pastors and ushers worked as best they could to drag the demonized to the rear of the platform, but there were just too many people possessed by devils. I knew that the power of God was present to heal and to deliver, just like in Luke 5:17. Ministering in the gifts of the word of knowledge and the word of wisdom, I began to call out healing after healing and miracle after miracle! The new converts began to literally throw the demonized people on to the platform! I commanded this to stop, but they continued to throw people on to the platform anyway. The meeting seemed to be spiraling out of control! The awe-inspiring, reverential power of God was being poured out! I did not know what to do next. So I decided to follow the leading of the Holy Spirit; that is always a great idea!

For a few moments things got a bit out of hand. I like to keep order on the platform; and I was trying to get some of the people, whom I knew had been healed, to come to the platform and give their testimonies. However, they just kept throwing people on the platform. Suddenly, I realized they were throwing the ones who had been healed on to the platform. Blind eyes had opened, deaf ears had been opened, and tumors had dissolved. There were people all over the place. "Bishop," I bellowed, "What are these three men doing on the platform? I only want those who are healed up here!"

"They can hear!" he replied. "What do you mean?" I asked. "These three men could not hear. They were, for sure, totally deaf. But now, sir, praise God, they do hear well!" We started to get the three deaf men's testimonies whom Jesus had sovereignly healed, when out of the corner of my eye something caught my attention. By now, the people were screaming and miracles were happening all over the crusade grounds. Thousands had just been saved and the power of God was now present to heal anyone willing to reach out and touch the hem of Jesus' garment. Jesus was sovereignly releasing mighty miracles and healings to the people of Beucelecelli. It seemed that the power of the age to come was visiting this little corner of Africa.

Frankenstein

Now I saw a man walking in my direction with both of his arms stretched out in front of him as if he were seeking to reach out and touch me. His appearance, and the way in which he was walking, made me feel quite uncomfortable. He was walking like the monster from one of those old *Frankenstein* movies. I saw him coming towards me from the other side of the platform, and I could see that he was having some trouble keeping his balance as he stepped over and between the writhing bodies that were littering the platform. In the back of my mind I remembered the pastors' warning from the previous night. Streams of tears were flowing from his eyes. "Bishop," I shrieked, "what is this guy doing up here?" pointing at the "Frankenstein" man. As the bishop spoke to him, I took a second to grab a drink of water and peek behind the platform where there were hundreds of people violently manifesting demons. Most of the pastors and ushers were busy with deliverance—in Swahili yelling and commanding the devils to come out.

This was the Kingdom of God manifest upon the earth! "Awesome!" I thought, "The Lord has manifested His glory and His great power and the kingdom of darkness is coming out of people! God's Kingdom has come!" I saw my friend, Wade Holland, sitting behind me; and I yelled at him over the din of noise, "Wade, get back there and cast out all those demons!" He seemed a little stunned, and he looked at me a little dumbfounded as if to say, "Me, cast out demons?" "Get back there," I ordered; and he jumped up and waded into the fray of writhing demonized people behind the platform.

The Levitating Woman

Wade did succeed in casting out a lot of devils that evening in the name of Jesus. However, later he told me that there was one woman whom he could not get delivered. She was levitating, or actually floating about eighteen inches off of the ground, and writhing like a snake. The whites of her eyes were red, and the pupils of her eyes were white. This poor woman's tongue appeared to be split as it poked in and out of her mouth like a serpent's tongue. I saw Wade later as the meeting was winding up. He sort of "walked" the levitating demonized woman around behind the platform with his hand on her throat commanding the devils within her to come out in Jesus' name.

Miracles were happening left and right and the power of God was being poured out in a very unusual way. Now the man who had been walking like Frankenstein was ready to give his testimony. I just handed the microphone to him, and he began to speak in Swahili and the bishop interpreted for me in English. The man said, "I was brought to the meeting today on my mat. As you know, I have been paralyzed from my birth. But when the white preacher said the words "the power of God is here to heal," I felt something like lightening go into my head. Power went into my body, my legs became strong, and I said to myself, 'For sure, Jesus has healed me.' You all know me, but as you can plainly see now, it is true. God has healed me and I can walk! Praise God! I can walk. Jesus is alive for He has healed me!"

The testimony that I was later given was that the man was well-known in the city. Many people did, indeed, know who he was. As he shared his testimony, the miracles began to multiply, and it seemed the faith of the people had exploded. It seemed as if the power of God multiplied yet again. Along with their faith, came an explosion of miracles! Healing after healing, miracle after miracle manifested. I did not touch anyone. The power of God was, indeed, present to heal. There were hundreds who were healed and hundreds who received miracles.

This was the most powerful single healing meeting I have ever personally witnessed. What Jesus did that day in Beucelecelli was truly amazing. God is worthy of all the glory!

I touched no one; Jesus Christ healed them all by His finished work of Calvary and through His shed blood! Was this a foreshadow and a taste of the powers of the age to come (Hebrews 6:5)? I have pondered the power of the Kingdom of Heaven that was released in Beucelecelli that day for many years. This incident initiated a radical search for answers to this question and mystery of heaven in my life. In the next chapter I will look at a few short testimonies of how the Lord is continuing to release the powers of the age to come even today.

CHAPTER 20

Pentecostal Power

On Thursday, May 16, 2013, Kathy and I were visiting Paul and Donna Cox in Hesperia, California. It was the season of Pentecost. During our visit and fellowship, I was explaining to Paul how we had been experiencing God's sovereign power. This phenomenon started about a decade ago in 2005 and had radically increased in our recent meetings. In fact, this phenomenon had accelerated since Labor Day week-end 2012. Since that time we have noticed that there is a greater release and level of the power of God being manifested in our meetings.

Many people have been experiencing unusual manifestations of the Spirit. People have often been "stuck" or "frozen" in one place for extended periods of time. Others have been having their spiritual eyes open to both see and hear into the spiritual realm. More and more people are being baptized with the Holy Spirit with the evidence of speaking in other tongues (Acts 2:3-4). Many people have reported seeing and hearing God's angels as they are manifesting around us as we are ministering or preaching. Lots of people attending the meetings are experiencing and smelling the fragrances of heaven. The miracles, signs, and wonders God is releasing are multiplying exponentially. I believe that they are multiplying all over the earth as the triumphant return of Jesus Christ draws neigh.

Orlando, Florida

We have had numerous mature believers have supernatural experiences, which I suppose could most accurately be referred to as trances in our meetings. Most of these people have had life changing encounters with the Kingdom of God and its King. Several people have reported seeing and speaking to the Lord Jesus Christ in our meetings. In Orlando, Florida, one man, a member of a government agency, was touched by the power of God as he stepped near Kathy and me as we were ministering. He later sent us his testimony. He stated that he not been "slain in the spirit" for over fifty years. Yet, when he stepped near the power that was hovering near us, his spiritual eyes were opened and he began to see God's angels all around (the seer anointing activated in his life). He said that he actually saw a spiritual door open and angelic beings coming in and go out of this supernatural opening or gate.

When this happened he went out in the spirit. (What some refer to as being slain in the Spirit.) During that time he began to weep and moan intensely in the natural realm. We were ministering in the Victorious Living Fellowship Church, and it was not their protocol to allow grown men to weep on the floor. However, at my suggestion they allowed this man to remain "in the spirit" on the carpet for about two hours. He was horizontal with the power of the Lord ministering to him sovereignly. This gentleman was totally undone when he finally stood to his feet later in the evening. He testified several days later that he had been taken into the pit of hell. There we witnessed the lake of fire and other horrendous places (ungodly dimensions).

He stated that he saw how the demonic beings tormented those in hell by plucking out their eyes and pulling off their arms and extremities. He said that he could smell the demonic stench and could hear the screams of those who were being tormented for eternity. This experience lasted for over an hour until Jesus appeared to this man telling him, *"Now that you have experienced hell, would you like to see heaven?"* The Lord then took this man to the heavenly realms and took him on a tour of the different places in heaven (godly dimensions). The man reported that he saw people he recognized in heaven, and after an extended tour of the heavenly places the Lord spoke to him again.

Jesus commissioned him and charged him to return to the earth and to *"tell the people that hell is a real place, but so is Heaven. Tell them what you have seen and experienced."* This man was so impacted by this experience that he was "under the influence" of the Holy Spirit for about a week. Currently he is struggling with the decision to leave his current job with a government agency and to launch out into itinerate ministry to *"tell the people what you have seen and experienced."*

Peoria, Illinois

On April 13, 2012, at the Conference on the Holy Spirit at the Bradley Epworth Church in Peoria, Illinois, a United Methodist Pastor had a similar experience when he testified that he had felt his heart "strangely warmed" by the power of the Holy Spirit. He later wrote to us and gave us the following testimony about this supernatural encounter with the power of God.

Kevin and his wife, Kathy, began asking anyone at the service to come forward and experience the open heavens, because it had been revealed to him that one opening was present in the room. When it was my turn, I started walking forward towards Kevin, and Kathy discerned where the spiritual gate or the opening was located. A few feet away from the opening, I felt a coldness come over my body. That was very strange, since it was actually warm in the room, too warm for the sweatshirt I was wearing. I started to take another step, when God opened my spirit eyes and I saw a mass of people walking around outside in a state of hopelessness. I started to cry and my legs felt weak. I couldn't take another step closer to the "opening."

Then my eyes were opened and I saw an orphanage where there were rows and rows of beds with children in them. As I looked at the beds, the children were crying and reaching out with their arms and hands as if they wanted me to hold them to my chest. I remember falling on my face and telling God to show me no more, that I couldn't take this anymore.

I asked the Lord to stop this. I was just overwhelmed with the tragedies of this world. I saw no one helping these people. All they seemed to want was someone to care. I tried to get up off the floor, but I was not able to move yet. Then God had me look down upon a huge mass of people who were wearing labels. They were placed at the fringe of a cliff and outside a walled city. I asked God who these people were. He said they were people, men and women, that society has forgotten, and to read their labels. I saw words like, "No self-esteem, divorce, anger, child or spousal abuse, severe grieving, uneducated, poverty, and neglect."

There were so many of these people. There was not a spot anywhere to stand. God lowered me to the earth, but I kept saying there are too many for me to help. I begged Him to stop showing me these things because I was only one person and could not deal with all the people. As I was finally able to open my eyes to the surroundings in the sanctuary, Kevin asked me if I still wanted to walk through the "opening." I told him that I definitely wanted to, but my legs and feet would not move. They were so weak that I couldn't even crawl through the spiritual door.

I remember two guys said they would lift me and drag me through if I wanted. I agreed, and as I crossed through, Kevin told the people that I had received a double portion. Then these two men dragged me to a chair so I could sit. It was at this time that I realized that I had sweated through both of my shirts. I had a large U-shaped wet spot on the front, and the whole back of my shirt was sweat through. One of the people there said that my face was "beet red."

I had to sit there for about 15 minutes before I had enough strength to get back to my seat. I immediately wrote in my journal about the experience. God has revealed since this happened that my calling in my ministry is to all these that He showed me. I will always have these people before me and He will help to point them out to me wherever I go. The very next day, He laid on my heart a family who needed groceries, and 3 days later, a lady at Wednesday night worship who needed some money for an upcoming expense that she did not know about yet. God also provided the finances for me to do those acts of kindness.

North Carolina

At one of our Summer Schools of the Supernatural an evangelist from West Virginia had an encounter with Jesus. She wrote us to say:

During a soaking time with the Lord while the glory of the Lord was still in the room after Kathy spoke about intimacy with the Lord, I had a visit to heaven where Jesus came and took me by the hand into Heaven with Him. I just kept seeing us go up and up and then we entered into this light and the sound was alive and I fell to my knees and I observed this white robe come over me and Jesus spoke to me and He said, "Today you have received what you have come for. I will speak to you and you will hear and you will do the greater works that I have called you to do. I will make connections for you, this is your time."

Then Jesus looked to the Father and they were talking but I couldn't make out what they were saying. And then I heard the Father ask me if I was ready to really be His Bride now? "YES"! Jesus took my hand stood me up and when I turned around I had an ephod on me with jewels and a crown had been placed on my head with many jewels. So I know that I received impartation of what the Lord had for me. I also received or was made more aware that an angel of God that was assigned to me"!

It is a very exciting God-ordained time. This time in School of the Supernatural and experiencing intimacy with the Lord has changed everything! Ministry doors are supernaturally opening for me and there is a great increase in the favor that the Lord has placed upon my ministry. Wonderful things have been happening really fast since the class at the School of the Supernatural. I have a confidence to know that I am where God wants me to be. Doors opening because the Heavens have been opened over my life!

Transformed by the Power of God

These kinds of supernatural experiences are only increasing and we can only share a few in this book, but there have been many encounters with the Kingdom of God like these recently. People's lives are being changed and transformed by the power of God, but I am aware that this is not the power or anointing of the Holy Spirit alone. So the question remains, what kind of power of God is this? These were the kinds of things Paul and I were discussing on Friday, May 15th, when we experienced a powerful visitation of the Kingdom of Heaven. During this encounter the Lord began to speak to us about the power that was being released in these kinds of meetings and experiences as I have just described.

This is not necessarily the power of the Holy Spirit, but rather the power of the whole Trinity. In the next chapter I will look at this dynamic and explore this power of heaven that we have been discerning. Could it be that this is an aspect of the powers of the age to come?

CHAPTER 21

What Are the Powers of the Age to Come?

It was during our visit with Paul and Donna Cox in Hesperia, California, that we experienced a visitation of heaven. In fact, I had been speaking to Paul and sharing with him many of the testimonies that I have shared in this book. I consider Paul to be a good friend, and I was seeking to have some wisdom or understanding from him. Surely, there is wisdom in a multitude of counselors.

Suddenly it seemed that the heavens opened and the glory and presence of God invaded Paul's living room. Henry seemed to move very quickly (for him) to a hiding place. (Henry is Paul and Donna's African tortoise). It was apparent that God had released a heavenly messenger to answer our questions and our prayers about the power of God that we had been discussing.

This heavenly messenger (spiritual being) spoke to us both very clearly telling us that the answer was to be found in Matthew 26:64. My first thought was that I am not familiar with that verse. Here is what Matthew 26: 64 says: *"Jesus said to him, 'It is as you said. Nevertheless, I say to you, hereafter you*

*will see the Son of Man sitting at the right hand of the Power,
and coming on the clouds of heaven."*

Suddenly we realized that this scripture held the answer to
the question we were asking the Lord. Suddenly I realized that
this was the answer to the question I had been asking the Lord
for since 2005. Jesus is sitting at the right hand of the Father.
Hebrews 12:2 makes this fact clear" *"Looking unto Jesus, the
author and finisher of our faith, who for the joy that was set
before Him endured the cross, despising the shame, and has sat
down at the right hand of the throne of God."*

Is it possible that one aspect of the powers of the age to
come includes the power of the Father and the power of the
Trinity? I believe that it does, and I believe that there is a
power and glory that all three of the Godhead exudes. There
is a glory of the Son. There is a glory of the Holy Spirit. And
there is certainly a glory of the Father. I have personally experienced the Father's glory at times on the earth and also in the
heavenly realms. Of course! The power indicated in Matthew
26:64 is the power of the Father, in my opinion. Perhaps this
heavenly dynamic is the power of the heavenly Father working
in perfect harmony with the anointing and power of the Holy
Spirit upon the earth together?

Later I fasted and prayed about this encounter in Hesperia and asked the Lord to show me another reference to the
power of the Father. The Lord directed me to the passage from
John 14:12. I had read this passage hundreds of times. Jesus
has said, *"Most assuredly, I say to you, he who believes in Me, the
works that I do he will do also; and greater works than these he
will do, because I go to My Father."*

I asked the Lord about this passage. *"How do we do the greater works* (miraculous deeds)?" The Lord spoke to me and told me that to do the greater works we needed to do them the same way Jesus did them and the Spirit said the key is in the passage. I searched and I searched and then I saw it! Look at what Jesus said in verse 10: *"Do you not believe that I am in the Father, and the Father in Me? The words that I speak to you I do not speak on My own authority; but the Father who dwells in Me does the works."*

Of course! Jesus plainly said that He did not do the works. I had always assumed that it was the anointing of the Holy Spirit that did the works and miracles in Jesus' ministry. But this verse plainly said, *"The Father who dwells in Me does the works."* This was speaking about the same power of the Father that we were supernaturally instructed to read from Matthew 26:64: *"I say to you, hereafter you will see the Son of Man sitting at the right hand of the Power, and coming on the clouds of heaven."* The Father is *the Power*!

This was a hidden key. This revelation was a hidden mystery revealed about the powers of the age to come. For over a decade I had never heard this concept taught. All that I had ever known was the power and the anointing of the Holy Spirit. Surely, Jesus was anointed with the power of the Holy Spirit and ministered in the gifts and anointing of the Holy Spirit (Acts 10:38). In fact, the scripture tells us that Jesus ministered in the power of the Holy Spirit without measure (John 3:31-36). Thank God for the power and the anointing of the Holy Spirit. But, I am now sure that the power of the Father was possibly the thing that I had been searching for.

The power of the Father must have certainly played a role in all of those times that unusual levels of God's power and glory had manifested like in Tanzania and in North Carolina and in Illinois and in Florida.

It's Supernatural!

At this point I want to share a recent encounter that I experienced with the power of the Holy Spirit. Kathy and I had traveled to Maricopa, Arizona, to minister with Patricia King and the XP Media team at the School of the Seers and the Supernatural. During this season I was pondering the material in this book with a lot of prayer and fasting. I was really seeking the Lord's heart concerning the idea that the Father was releasing a new level of Kingdom power. Of course, I am referring to the power of the Father. You see, this has been an ongoing mystery in my life.

I have been seeking the Lord for revelation and understanding about the amazing outpourings of His power and His Spirit since I saw the little girl raised from the dead in Tanzania. I had finalized this book prior to leaving Moravian Falls on the way to Arizona, but in my spirit there was still a knowing that there was a missing piece to the book. Writing a book is a lot like giving birth to a child (of course I am using an analogy here)! However, in the spirit I sensed that the water had broken and the book was coming forth into this world quickly. As any mother can tell you, it is an uncomfortable sensation when your water breaks, a combination of wondrous expectancies combined with a little trepidation and awe.

While we were in Maricopa I received an email from Sid Roth's ministry. It was an opportunity to attend one of Sid's new mentoring sessions with Pastor Benny Hinn. When I read the email my heart leaped and I immediately accepted the invitation to attend the taping of the program in Charlotte, North Carolina. The taping and mentoring session was to be Tuesday, January 27, at 3 p.m. at the It's Supernatural Network studios. Because I have appeared on Sid's program in the past, I was able to ask his assistant if I could come into the studio a little early and avoid the waiting line. Sid's staff was very gracious to Kathy and me, and arranged for us to come early.

We flew in from Arizona and almost immediately turned around to drive to Charlotte for the mentoring session with Pastor Benny Hinn. We arrived just in the nick of time. When we arrived at the studio, we just had time to grab a bite to eat and then walk into the VIP doors. As we walked in, Tia was calling our name and we were taken to the front of the line. In just a moment or two we were ushered into the closed set for the taping of the program with Pastor Benny Hinn. My life was transformed by the ministry of Benny Hinn going back to 1982. Again in 2001, Pastor Benny's book *Good Morning Holy Spirit* was used by the Lord to make the person of the Holy Spirit *REAL* to me! (I have written about that experience in the book *Unlocking the Hidden Mysteries of the Seer Anointing II: The Blessings of Psalm 24*). So I was pregnant with expectation for this mentoring session!

As we walked into the studio at ISN, I felt the powerful glory of God. I felt the presence of the Holy Spirit in a fresh and pristine way. I began to weep, but sought to hold my emotions in check. There was a season in my life when the presence and person of the Holy Spirit had been very real and tangible to me. As I closed my eyes, I began to sense and feel the person of the Holy Spirit washing over me in waves just as I had experienced Him in 2001 and 2002. During that season the Holy Spirit seemed to accompany me everywhere that I went. I was elated, to say the least. Tia had Kathy and I move to the far end of the front row of the studio, and as I sat down I felt the presence and power of the Holy Spirit begin to swell and fill the studio. I was praising God for this evening and it had not even begun. Thank you, Lord, for the Holy Ghost!

I closed my eyes and relished and luxuriated in the power and the presence of the person of the Holy Spirit. There were announcements and instructions given to the studio audience prior to the taping of the program with Pastor Benny and Sid. Inwardly I was relishing the glory and the person of the Holy Spirit, whom I sensed in a great and mighty way. I closed my eyes and rested in the presence and glory of the Holy Spirit that was hanging thickly in the atmosphere of the studio. It seemed to me that the atmosphere of heaven had fallen at ISN. Suddenly I felt an increase of the presence and glory of the Holy Spirit. I opened my eyes to look to my left and standing about fifteen feet from Kathy and me was Pastor Benny. He was smiling and seemed to be greatly enjoying himself.

I remembered how Pastor Benny's teaching on the Holy Spirit had helped me as a new Spirit-filled believer. Now, here—this fourteen years later, I was about to be taught about the Holy Spirit again by Pastor Benny personally along with the studio audience. I was ecstatic. Once the program began and Pastor Benny was seated at the desk of the *It's Supernatural* set with Sid Roth and as the program started, the presence of the Holy Spirit seemed to greatly increase. Pastor Benny was only around eighteen feet from where we were sitting. It was a wonderful program.

After the taping, Pastor Benny began to teach the studio audience secrets about his relationship with the person of the Holy Spirit. A round table was brought out, and Pastor Benny taught from the table just about five or ten feet away from me. I was rapt by Pastor Benny's teaching and understanding of the person of the Holy Spirit. He taught us for about ninety minutes. It was glorious! As Pastor Benny taught and spoke, the power and presence of the Holy Spirit began to move upon my heart and within my spirit. When the teaching was concluded, Pastor Benny announced that he was going to minister to us. By now I was really being touched by the Holy Spirit. I was stirred by the message and was hungry for more of the Holy Spirit in my life. Pastor Benny led us in several worship songs.

As we worshiped the Lord, the power and anointing of the Holy Spirit fell upon me in wave after wave. I was lost in worship. I was lost in the presence and the power of the Holy Spirit. I was experiencing the person of the Holy Spirit in a fresh and new way that I had not experienced for nearly fifteen years. Tears filled my eyes and flowed down my cheeks as we worshiped the Lord in the presence of the Holy Spirit. I was lost in worship of the Person of the Holy Spirit in spirit and in truth. I forgot about the people around me and the fact that cameras were rolling and recording the meeting. I was just undone by the power and the person of the Holy Spirit. It was glorious, and I did not want for the evening to end!

Soon Pastor Benny began to minister to people. I was under the influence of the Spirit and actually did not realize Pastor Benny was praying for those next to me until he prayed for Kathy, my wife. Then he prayed for me, and the power of the Holy Spirit really touched me in a glorious and magnificent way. I was now under the heavy weighty power, anointing, and glory of the person of the Holy Spirit. I remember being called up to stand in a line, and Pastor Benny prayed for me a second time. This time the power of God was even greater than the first time, and I was slain in the Spirit (I fell as if unconscious on the studio floor). The power and glory of God that rested upon me after Pastor Benny prayed for me the second time was incredible. This was similar to the time that Jesus had stood over me and prayed for my left hand on November 25, 2001.

I remember that about four men tried to help me to stand up so that Pastor Benny could pray for the next line of people. But they had a difficult time lifting me off the floor, as I seemed to be supernaturally heavy. The men managed to take me back to my seat on the front row. I was undone, and the power and the presence of the Holy Spirit were resting upon me in a glorious fashion. Suddenly I heard Pastor Benny say; "Where is that man?" I remembered thinking, "I wonder who he is talking about?" It turns out he was speaking about me. "Bring him back up here." Once again the four men carried me to stand in front of Pastor Benny. Pastor Benny then spoke to me, asking me who I was. He asked me, "Are you a pastor?" I was so heavily under the glory and power of the Holy Spirit that I just smiled and said, "No, I am just a friend of God."

I remember Pastor Benny laughing and saying, "I like that; but are you a minister?" Then Sid Roth came up and stood beside Pastor Benny and told him that I was a minister. Pastor Benny then spoke several words of encouragement over my life and laid his hands upon me again to pray for impartation. He said, "The world needs to see the miracle working power of God. The Lord wants you to use this anointing that He has placed upon you to pray for miracles. Do you understand?" It seemed that lightening struck me on the top of my head when Pastor Benny laid his hands upon me the third time. The glory of God and the power of the Holy Spirit once more coursed through my body, and I was again down on the black studio floor in the ISN studio with what seemed to be rivers of the power and anointing of the Holy Spirit washing through me in wave after wave. I was undone and was not able to physically move my body an inch. Pastor Benny continued to pray for many more people, but I was now somewhere else. I was now engulfed and energized by the power of the person of the Holy Spirit.

The power of the Holy Spirit continues to wash over and course through my body in waves even weeks after this experience. About thirty minutes later I scrambled out of the studio of ISN and the power and presence of the person of the Holy Spirit seemed to walk out with me. Kathy and I returned to Moravian Falls, and I immediately headed into my little prayer room to rest in the presence and power of the Holy Spirit. You see, my heart's prayer was not to grieve the Holy Spirit with the material that I have written in this book. I honor the Holy Spirit. I need the Holy Spirit. I want more of the Holy Spirit, and I have no desire to in any way diminish the power and ministry of the person of the Holy Spirit, or to negate the vital ministry of the Holy Spirit at all.

He is real to me. The Holy Spirit is the agent of revival that is moving over the earth at this hour. Perhaps, in His sovereignty, the Lord allowed me to once again encounter the Person of the Holy Spirit in the same measure that I met Him in 2001. During that season the Holy Spirit was more real to me that the book you are holding in your hands. He was my companion, and the precious Holy Spirit was and is my Friend. Therefore, I want to make it clear that the power of the Father and the powers of the age to come will in no way, shape, or fashion replace the precious Holy Spirit.

No, the Holy Spirit will have an eminent and pivotal role in the release of the power of the Father that I believe is being released from the heavenly realms onto the earth as the return of Christ draws neigh. Ecclesiastes 4:12 teaches us that: *A threefold cord is not quickly broken.*

I believe that what Pastor Benny spoke over me is the Father's heart and desire for everyone reading this book. The Lord wants the power and miracles of God to be poured out through you just as Pastor Benny prophesied: "*The world needs to see the miracle working power of God. The Lord wants you to use the power and the anointing of the Holy Spirit that He has placed upon you to pray for miracles. The world needs to see the miracle working power of God.*" Please take these inspired words as a prophetic word for you!

Perhaps the powers of the age to come will be an incredible work of the Trinity as the power of God is released from the very throne of the Father in threefold liberation of the power and glory of God the Father, God the Son, and God the Holy Spirit. The fact is, we know in part and we prophesy in part (1 Corinthians 13:9-13). I believe that there is a Power that is about to invade the earth from the heavenly realms that will help to usher in the great last days harvest. Perhaps it is the Power that Jesus Himself prophesied of in Matthew 26:64: "*It is as you said. Nevertheless, I say to you, hereafter you will see the Son of Man sitting at the right hand of the Power, and coming on the clouds of heaven.*"

Perhaps *the Power* described in this passage *is* the Power of the Father or Eloheim? Perhaps, the precious Holy Spirit will be loosed in a tangible way upon the earth that we have not dreamed possible up to now? After all we have such exceedingly great promises from our heavenly Father. But, as it is written: "*Eye has not seen, nor ear heard, Nor have entered into the heart of man The things which God has prepared for those who love Him*" (1 Corinthians 2:9).

One aspect of the powers of the age to come is the power of heaven that is released by the Father as He decrees judgments of truth from His throne of mercy and grace. In the next chapter I will summarize the correlation between the powers of the age to come, the eminent release of the Power of the Father, and the shaking that is unfolding upon the earth at this hour.

CHAPTER 22

The Shaking Will Continue

Starting about one week before the Heaven Touching Earth #5 School of the Seers, I began to experience an unusual phenomenon. The earth began to quake and shake under my feet. I became aware that the ground and the earth were shifting. As I sought the Lord about this, I was well aware that this shifting was not only in the natural realm but also there is a real shaking in the spiritual realm.

In fact, the quaking became so strong during the Heaven Touching Earth #5 School of the Seers that I mentioned it to Paul Cox. Paul had traveled from California to North Carolina to minister at the event. He also confirmed that he began to feel not only the earth move but also the heavens shake when he arrived in Moravian Falls. As the meetings progressed this shaking and quaking became more intense. At one point as I was preparing to move from the green room into the conference meeting on Saturday, August 31, 2013, at 6:38 p.m., when the shaking seemed to literally shake the building and the entire hotel.

I moved from the bathroom to look at the curtains in the living room area and there was a noticeable sway in the material of the curtains. It also seemed as if the carpet under my feet was shifting and moving in sync to a heavenly sound. It seemed to me that the whole earth was resonating and the heavens seemed to open up a little more at that moment. I believe that there is a definite correlation between the heavenly sound and the shakings that we were experiencing.

Later when I mentioned this to Paul Cox he confirmed that he also discerned a literally shaking of the earth and a heavenly harmonic sound. The release of this supernatural sound seemed to be causing the shaking, resonating, and quaking. In fact, Paul mentioned this shaking phenomenon to Don Potter who was leading worship and Don showed Paul a device that detects sound. From the readings from the device, it appeared that there was indeed a harmonic resonation that was being released into the atmosphere of the region. Don's device actually measured the movement and shaking scientifically according to Paul Cox's testimony.

Usually the Lord will begin to position me and alert me to supernatural phenomenon as we approach the Day of Atonement. So as these events were unfolding, the shaking of the grounds seemed to only increase exponentially during the Heaven Touching Earth #5 School of the Seers. In fact, the shaking continued after the meetings and the grounds seemed to swell and tremble here in Moravian Falls after the event. I began to become aware that there was a heavenly sound that was, I believe, actually coming from the bowels of the earth. I suppose one could more accurately say that the earth was resonating or groaning. However, this same harmonic sound also seemed to be emanating from the heavenly realms or dimensions.

As I sought the Lord about this in prayer, the Holy Spirit dropped this scripture into my heart from Romans 8:19-22:

> *For the earnest expectation all of creation eagerly waits for the revealing of the sons of God. For the creation was subjected to futility, not willingly, but because of Him who subjected it in hope; because the creation itself also will be delivered from the bondage of corruption into the glorious liberty of the children of God. For we know that the whole creation groans and labors with birth pangs together until now.*

I believe that the Lord is allowing those who are mature and who have developed their ability to discern supernatural phenomenon to hear the earth as it is literally groaning and laboring as a woman who is in labor at this hour. Incidentally, the School of the Seers was held on Labor Day weekend; and the Lord had promised supernatural things to be birthed including ministries, destinies, and revelations! This book, for example, was birthed during this season.

Groaning in Georgia

After the School of the Seers, Kathy and I traveled to Sedona, Arizona, to minister. We were at the New Beginnings Festival that was held on Rosh Hashanah 2013. The festival, which was sponsored by David Herzog Ministries, began in the evening of Wednesday, September 4, and ended in the evening of Friday,

September 6, 2013. I was astonished to feel the earth trembling as I disembarked at Hartsfield-Jackson International Airport in Atlanta, Georgia. In fact, it seemed that I could hear the earth groaning in Georgia. Later on the flight from Atlanta to Phoenix, Arizona, I sought the Lord concerning these things.

Once again, as I soared at 30,000 feet across America, I felt the heavens shaking yet again. I discerned the same harmonic resonance and heavenly sound. I asked the Lord what was He doing, and at that exact second the entire plane was jarred with turbulence and literally shook and trembled just as I have felt the earth shake in North Carolina and in Georgia. The Lord spoke to me very clearly in that instant and declared that He was once again shaking the heavens and the earth!

Instantly, I was launched into a vision and I saw the throne room again. I saw the glory of God as it vaulted through the heavenly courts and around the throne of the Father. The Father was speaking through the glory. Suddenly I saw His mighty right hand descend down through the midst of the glory. The Father smacked the podium of His throne with a massive wooden gavel sending lightning and thunder shooting from the throne of God. The Father's gavel was ornately made with brilliant filigree inlay designs in the mallet. It thundered in the heavenly realms and seemed to shake the earth when the gavel struck the material of the Father's throne. The plane was flying through thunder clouds at that time, and it seemed that the plane shook in symphony with the heavens.

His Mercy Endures Forever

The Father was speaking and these words echoed in my spirit; *"Yet once more I shake not only the earth, but also heaven."* Somehow I understood that this experience and shaking were a foretaste of the things that the Lord was going to show to me on the Day of Atonement. Thunder shook the air and lightening lit up the skies outside. Once again the Lord stirred up my spirit to ponder the scriptures from Hebrews 12 that He had highlighted when the earth first began to shake in Moravian Falls. Surely there is a shaking coming, and a hard rain is going to fall.

Hebrews 12:25-29

See that you do not refuse Him who speaks. For if they did not escape who refused Him who spoke on earth, much more shall we not escape if we turn away from Him who speaks from heaven, whose voice then shook the earth; but now He has promised, saying, "Yet once more I shake not only the earth, but also heaven." Now this, "Yet once more," indicates the removal of those things that are being shaken, as of things that are made, that the things which cannot be shaken may remain. Therefore, since we are receiving a kingdom which cannot be shaken, let us have grace, by which we may serve God acceptably with reverence and godly fear. For our God is a consuming fire.

The Father Is Good

Our Father is a merciful God and His mercy endures forever. We need to understand He is the God of both the heavenly realms and the earth and dimensions. He is faithful, the Lord keeps His covenants with His children, and His mercy endures for a thousand generations with those who love Him and keep His commandments. The Father is good and His mercy is everlasting. It is eternal, and His truth endures to all generations.

However, we must also remember that He repays those who hate Him to destroy them. God will not be slack with those who hate Him. The Lord will repay those who hate His ways to their face. This aspect of God's righteous judgments is true for individuals, for counties, for states, for nations, and even the whole earth.

We have entered into a season when the God of the universe is speaking from His throne of mercy and grace. His voice is thundering from the heavenly realms, and as a result the heavens and the earth are quivering and shaking. Even the spiritual dimensions are shaking and the veil between heaven and earth is becoming more and more porous. Yet, in all of this, for those who love the Lord and are called according to His purposes we can rejoice. For the righteous judgments of God are His mercy. For the righteous judgments of God lead men to repentance. We must remember that the righteous judgments of God are the riches of His goodness, forbearance, and longsuffering. We must realize that the shaking that is accelerating upon the earth is the goodness of God, which will lead many people to repentance. The shaking will motivate people to return to the Lord.

It is a season to try our own hearts and to submit to the Spirit of the Most High God. For the Creator of the heavens and the earth is speaking from His throne of mercy and grace. However, we must remember that the Father's throne is also a throne of judgment. We must remember that the righteous judgments of God are His goodness. Truly, it is a fearful thing to fall into the hands of the living God (Hebrews 10:31). God's voice is shaking the earth, and even the earth recognizes the voice of the Creator and yearns and groans for the restoration of the Kingdom of Heaven upon the earth. All of creation shouts for the Creator to return. Even the trees and stones are shouting out, "Holy, holy, holy!" The entire earth is trembling with earnest expectation. In fact, you can Google "the earth is groaning" to find dozens of videos on this supernatural phenomenon on the internet, including an amazing recording of the earth groaning in Kiev, Ukraine, and Windsor, Ontario, Canada and various other places on the earth!

God Is Shaking the Nations

"Yet once more I shake not only the earth, but also heaven" (Hebrews 12:26).

The Lord is speaking from His throne of mercy and grace. He is speaking from His throne of judgments, and the Father is shaking the nations of the earth. God's hosts have gone forth with the plum line in their hands. Zechariah 4 is the season that we have entered at this hour. That is why there is so much turmoil and distress in the nations of the earth at this hour. Yet in all of these things, God will keep those in perfect peace whose minds are stayed upon Him (Isaiah 26:3).

Zechariah 4: 8-14

Moreover the word of the LORD came to me, saying: "The hands of Zerubbabel Have laid the foundation of this temple; His hands shall also finish it. Then you will know That the LORD of hosts has sent Me to you. For who has despised the day of small things? For these seven rejoice to see The plumb line in the hand of Zerubbabel. They are the eyes of the LORD, Which scan to and fro throughout the whole earth." Then I answered and said to him, "What are these two olive trees—at the right of the lampstand and at its left?" And I further answered and said to him, "What are these two olive branches that drip into the receptacles of the two gold pipes from which the golden oil drains?" Then he answered me and said, "Do you not know what these are?" And I said, "No, my lord." So he said, "These are the two anointed ones, who stand beside the Lord of the whole earth."

God Is Shaking the Heavens

Even the heavens are being stirred up, and the Lord is releasing the host of heaven to invade the earthly realms and dimensions. There will be a great acceleration of angelic activity upon the earth. Many people will begin to see and discern the angelic hosts of heaven as they invade our spheres of influence.

Along with God's angelic beings, there will be a release of other supernatural beings from the heavenly realms. Some of these will be the anointed ones who stand beside the throne of the Father. There will be a manifestation and appearance of many of the great cloud of witnesses in the coming days. Remember that the Lord is not the God of the dead but the God of the living. That is what Jesus said in Matthew 22:32: *"'I am the God of Abraham, the God of Isaac, and the God of Jacob'? God is not the God of the dead, but of the living."*

We are entering into a time when Mount Zion, the city of the living God, the heavenly Jerusalem, an innumerable company of angels, and the general assembly and church of the firstborn who are registered in heaven, and the spirits of just men made perfect (Hebrews 12: 22-23) will begin to be released by the command of God to come and to manifest upon the earth. This innumerable company will be at the command of Christ and will help to prepare the way of the Lord as Jesus declared and prophesied in Matthew 24:29-31 (emphasis added):

> *Immediately after the tribulation of those days the sun will be darkened, and the moon will not give its light; the stars will fall from heaven, and **the powers of the heavens will be shaken**. Then the sign of the Son of Man will appear in heaven, and then all the tribes of the earth will mourn, and **they will see the Son of Man coming on the clouds of heaven with power and great glory. And He will send His angels with a great sound of a trumpet, and they will gather together His elect from the four winds, from one end of heaven to the other.***

Yes, the Father is speaking from his throne in the heavens and the earth is trembling and shaking. Even the heavenly realms are trembling as the powers of darkness, and the principalities and powers of darkness understand that their time is short. Soon there will be the sound of a trump, and the earth will shake, and the heavens will rip open to reveal the King of kings and the Lord of lords. Jesus will return in triumph and great glory with His angelic hosts and an innumerable company of angels, along with the general assembly and church of the firstborn who are registered in heaven (the great cloud of witnesses).

"Yet once more I shake not only the earth, but also heaven" (Hebrews 12:26).

The Father is speaking from His throne in the heavens and the earth is trembling and shaking. The Lord is sending the anointed ones that stand around the throne to measure the church. They have God's plumb line in their hands. Nothing will be hidden from the eyes of Almighty God. This is no longer a time for the church to be mired in mediocrity and complacency.

God Is Shaking the House of God

The Father is inspecting, weighing, and trying the heart of the church and will give to each one his just reward (Jeremiah 17:10). Jesus spoke about this dynamic of His triumphant return, saying, *"Behold, I am coming quickly, and My reward is with Me, to give to everyone according to his work"* (Revelation 22:12). It is a time to watch and pray (Mark 13:33). It is a time to prepare and to trim your wick (Matthew 25:7). The

Day of the Lord will come like a thief in the night (1 Thessalonians 5:2). Certainly no man knows the day or the hour (Mark 13:32). Yet, the earth trembles and shakes as the Day of the Lord draws neigh (Luke 21:25-28).

It does not take a prophet to see that God is once more shaking the heavens and the earth. Surely, the Lord will begin to shake the house of God at this hour. Surely the Lord will begin to test the hearts of men. For the time has come for judgment to begin at the house of God. Surely, the Father will begin to test and judge the Body of Christ first. And if God judges His people with righteous judgments, then what will be the end of those who do not obey the Gospel of God, and those who do not know God (1 Peter 4:17)?

> "Yet once more I shake not only the earth, but also heaven" (Hebrews 12:26).

God is shaking His people. God is shaking His church. God is shaking His Bride. Will she awake? Will she turn back to the Lord with all of her heart, with all of her soul, and with all of her mind? Will she put away her childish ways? Will she stop building the kingdom of man and realize that she is called to build the Kingdom of Heaven? Will she rise up and train and equip true sons and daughters of God? Will she begin to equip people to fulfill their God-ordained destiny instead of training people to serve the church and the crumbling kingdom of men?

Who Will Comprehend?

Yes, God is about to shake the church in a great and mighty way. Everything that has been built that was not ordained by

God may fall. Watch as the Lord begins to raise up and super-naturally equip the most unlikely and foolish people to preach the Gospel of the Kingdom with passion, power, and true God-ordained authority. Watch as the power of the Father will be seen among the nations of the earth and miracles, signs, and wonders will begin to mark the true and mature sons and daughters of the Most High God. Watch as the power of the Father and the Power of the Trinity will continue to shake the nations of the earth.

Watch as everything that can be shaken will be shaken as the Father of glory is thundering from His throne of mercy and grace. Watch as God begins to raise up the true church to whom the God of our Lord Jesus Christ, the Father of glory, will surely give the spirit of wisdom and revelation in the knowledge of Him—a remnant whose eyes of understanding will be enlightened, and who will have supernatural surety and clarity of the hope of their calling. Who will comprehend what are the riches of the glory of His inheritance in the saints (Ephesians 1:17-18).

These mature sons and daughters of the Most High God will know what is the exceeding greatness of the Father's power toward those of us who believe, according to the working of His mighty power (*ischus*, mighty; *kratos*, delegated dominion power; and *exousia*, delegated authority) which God worked in each of us through Christ when He raised Him from the dead and seated Him at His right hand in the heavenly places, far above all principality and power and might and dominion, and every name that is named, not only in this age but also in that which is to come. They will realize that the riches of the glory of the Father are in them. The power of the Father has placed all things under Christ's feet, and given Him to be head over all things to the church, which is His body, the fullness of Him who fills all in all in you (Ephesians 1:19-23).

Double Peace—Shalom, Shalom

As this shaking intensifies, know that as we die to ourselves and learn to become alive in Christ, we are receiving a Kingdom that cannot be shaken. No matter what transpires upon the earth. No matter to what extent the financial institutions of the world shake, crumble, and fail. No matter to what extent the governments of the world crumble and decay. You have an inheritance that can never be shaken. No matter what kinds of tribulation come. Even through famine, earthquakes, fear, fire, floods, chaos, rebellions, shortages, and the like, we are more than conquerors through Christ who strengthens us. For I am absolutely certain that neither death nor life, nor angels nor principalities nor powers, nor things present nor things to come, nor height nor depth, nor any other created thing, shall be able to separate us from the love of God which is in Christ Jesus our Lord (Romans 8:37-39).

Yes, there is a great shaking coming to the heavens, to the earth, and to the church. But for those who love the Lord and keep their minds focused upon Him, the Father will keep them in perfect shalom, shalom. God will keep us in perfect peace even though there is a shaking coming upon us (Isaiah 26:3). *"Therefore, since we are receiving a kingdom which cannot be shaken, let us have grace, by which we may serve God acceptably with reverence and godly fear"* (Hebrews 12:28).

The Lord will begin to make a way for those who love Him to overcome the storms and shakings that are to come. The Lord will begin to release the supernatural wisdom and revelation of His Kingdom to His children. God will begin to give His people the ability to overcome the world by understanding that the Kingdom of Heaven *is* real, and that His Kingdom and His power are truly at hand. We will understand the fact that we are receiving a Kingdom which cannot be shaken. Let me encourage you with these words of the Lord Jesus as you see and feel the shaking increasing: *"These things I have spoken to you, that in Me you may have peace. In the world you will have tribulation; but be of good cheer, I have overcome the world"* (John 16:33). This great shaking that has come upon to the heavens and upon the earth is a dynamic of the powers of the age to come.

Yes, it may be the end of the world as we know it, but you can be fine.

The Glorious Presence of Elohim

On September 14, 2013, I sat upon the white rocking chair looking at the manicured gardens at the iMAEC swaying like a wave in the evening sun. It was the day after my friend Per had called me from Stockholm, Sweden. It seemed as if a holy hush fell upon the new equipping center. Yom Kippur was now ending and the evening sun was beginning to filter through the mulberry tree and around the magnificent butterfly bushes. Golden monarchs drifted and glided in the heavenly evening light. The glory of God began to fall upon me in waves once more. It seemed as if the Father was smiling upon me, and tears of joy began to trickle from my eyes. In my heart this prayer came out:

> *Thank You, Lord, for You are good. You are very good to Your servant. Praise Your holy name, Lord; I praise Your wonderful name, Lord.*

Within my soul I was worshiping the Lord—the Lord who had given me such wonderful blessings and privileges. Even the flowers blooming all around me seemed to worship the Lord in spirit and in truth. Even the butterflies and the bees seemed to be worshiping God at that moment. Heaven invaded earth. I embraced this perfect peace and relished this instant of time. A holy hush resonated, and I realized that the earth was once more shaking beneath my feet. It was supernaturally quiet and still and in that instant the Lord spoke to me, saying, *"Yet once more I shake not only the earth, but also heaven."*

Revelation filled my spirit.

That is truly the season that we are entering at this hour.

The Creator of heaven and earth is releasing a shaking from His throne of mercy and grace. This shaking has been preordained before the foundations of the earth were laid. Everything that has been build on sand will fall, and the works of men will be judged soon. Most will be found lacking. Most of our works may be found to be hay, straw, and stubble (1 Corinthians 3:12-16).

The Creator of heaven and earth will soon release a holy consuming fire upon the earth and upon the sons of man.

Isaiah 5:24

Therefore, as the fire devours the stubble, And the flame consumes the chaff. So shall their root will be as rottenness, And their blossom will ascend like dust; Because they [the people of earth] have rejected the law of the LORD of hosts, And despised the word of the Holy One of Israel.

In the glory that flowed around me, the power of the heaven began to resonate and the ground continued to shake. It seemed that the heavens opened once more. Mount Zion seemed to come down upon me and the International Ministry Apostolic Equipping Center (iMAEC). An innumerable host of angelic beings seemed to ascend and descend onto the grounds. Heaven once more seemed to be touching earth. And I alone stood still to see the salvation of the Lord this beautiful day. I stood in awe of the heavenly realms that were invading my space as the Day of Atonement ended with a crescendo of the power and with the glorious presence of Elohim. I sensed the power and the pleasure of the Father.

It seemed as if the angels of the Lord were dancing and praising the Most High God on the grounds. The fragrances of heaven wafted around me and my spirit leaped with joy. Once more the carousel of heaven seemed to manifest. Spiritual gates and portals began to open in a similar fashion that they manifested at the School of the Seers #5 on September 1, 2013. It seemed as if the hosts of heaven were stepping into this dimension to tour the new iMAEC. This revelation made smile and my spirit seemed to soar a little higher. I sensed that the Father was leaning over the edge of heaven and smiling down upon me from His throne of mercy and grace.

Suddenly, in the spirit, a pillar of fire appeared. The glory of God multiplied and fiery angelic beings formed ranks around the consuming fire that was hovering nearby. It seemed as if the spirit of wisdom and revelation was present. I discerned the spirit of counsel and might. In addition to this the spirit of knowledge and of the fear of the Lord fell upon me and great trepidation came into my heart. I closed my eyes and prayed that I would not be consumed as the fire and glory of God instantly increased and seemed to burn within my spirit, soul, and body. This burning sensation lasted for several minutes.

During this time I was aware that innumerable angelic hosts were visiting the iMAEC. I discerned that many of the great cloud of witnesses were among those hosts of heaven that had come to visit and inspect the grounds of the equipping center too. The heavens opened and they were visiting me. God's angels were dancing and worshiping the Lamb of God! All of heaven seemed to rejoice and praise the Lord in unity and harmony. The sounds of heaven rang in my ears. The earth continued to vibrate and shake in symphony with the sounds of heaven. I could discern a marvelous heavenly harmonic sound, and this same supernatural resonance rang in my ears and in my spirit. I discerned a perfect sound that was resonating from the Father's throne at that moment. This supernatural sound resonated at a perfect pitch. I realized that the throne had come down. Heaven had come down to visit me here in the very heart of Moravian Falls!

From the midst of the all consuming fire, I heard the scriptures from Hebrews 12:22-24 declared:

> You have come to Mount Zion and to the city of the living God, the heavenly Jerusalem, to an innumerable company of angels, to the general assembly and church of the firstborn who are registered in heaven, to God the Judge of all, to the spirits of just men made perfect, to Jesus the Mediator of the new covenant, and to the blood of sprinkling that speaks better things than that of Abel.

These words began to resonate louder and appeared to cause the ground to shake even more intensely under my feet. Once more I heard the Spirit, declaring verses 25-29:

> *See that you do not refuse Him who speaks. For if they did not escape who refused Him who spoke on earth, much more shall we not escape if we turn away from Him who speaks from heaven, whose voice then shook the earth; But now He has promised, saying, "Yet once more I shake not only the earth, but also heaven." Now this, "Yet once more," indicates the removal of those things that are being shaken, as of things that are made, that the things which cannot be shaken may remain. Therefore, since we are receiving a kingdom which cannot be shaken, let us have grace, by which we may serve God acceptably with reverence and godly fear. For God is a consuming fire.*

The reverential fear of the Lord raced through my spirit. The grounds literally shook beneath my feet, and I feared to open my eyes least I might die. The winds of heaven began to swirl about me, and after a while it seemed as if the spirit of knowledge and of the fear of the Lord lifted. I continued to luxuriate in the glory of the Lord and listen to the sounds of heaven that were resonating and ringing all around me at that moment.

I understood that this shaking will come with unusual manifestations of the Kingdom of Heaven.

Yet in all of this shaking, God will keep His people in perfect peace who trust in Him and who keep their hearts focused upon him, as He tells us in Isaiah 26:3: *"You will keep him in* perfect peace, Whose mind is stayed on You, Because he trusts in You."

Yes, it is the end of the world as we know it.

Lord, help us to keep our minds focused upon you.

Still, there is no doubt that we will see a great increase of unusual releases and manifestations of the powers of the Kingdom of Heaven. There will be supernatural releases of the power of the Father. These manifestations will in no way replace the magnificent Holy Spirit or the wonderful gifts of the Spirit. No, they will augment the power and anointing of the Holy Spirit. In fact, the anointing of the Holy Spirit will play a crucial role in your ability to discern and minister in the powers of the age to come and in the power of the Father and of the Trinity.

There will be a release of the power of the Father, the power of the Son, and the power of the Holy Spirit in harmony and in tandem. These will be greater than anything that the earth has experienced up to now. Perhaps, the author of the Book of Hebrews prophesied about this imminent phenomenon referring to it as "*the good word of God and the powers of the age to come*" (6:5). The truth is no one will be able to articulate the power of God that the Creator of heaven and earth is prepared to release upon the earth. This is remains a hidden mystery of Heaven.

In 1 Corinthians 2:9 we read: "*It is written: 'Eye has not seen, nor ear heard, Nor have entered into the heart of man The things which God has prepared for those who love Him.*"

Perhaps, the powers of the age to come are at hand?

The whole earth is groaning and awaiting the manifestation of the Kingdom of God. As the glory lingered, the Holy Spirit whispered into my ear: *"For the earnest expectation of the creation eagerly waits for the revealing of the sons of God"* (Romans 8:19). As mature sons and daughters of God, we are receiving a Kingdom which cannot be shaken.

In the spirit many doors (spiritual gates) are opening. The key of David is being released to God's children at this hour to open doors and to shut doors (Isaiah 22:22). The Lord is opening doors (spiritual gates) that no man can shut and closing other doors that no man can open. What a glorious time to be alive!

The Kingdom of Heaven is truly at hand.

The time has come for the manifestation of the true sons and daughters of the Most High God.

"They are coming," says the Lord. "My chosen ones are arising even now. They will not look like what many expect. No, I will raise up the most unlikely," says the Lord. "The discarded, the forgotten, the broken, the hopeless, the least likely; these will be my jewels. These I will endue with heavenly power and revelation. I will use them in unusual power and demonstrations of My Spirit and of My Kingdom. They are coming, even now. These mature sons and daughters of the Most High God are arising! The rulers of this age are passing away, and a new generation is arising to take their place. They will walk in holiness and with My authority. They will rise up into the heavenlies and see and hear what must take

place after this. They shall bring the wisdom of men to nothing and the foolishness of this age will be destroyed. The Kingdom of God shall arise and the kingdom of man shall tumble and fall. The shaking is coming! The shaking is coming! No one can hide from the wrath that is to come. Only in Me is there safety and salvation," says the Lord. "Seek Me while I may still be found. Seek Me before the end is come."

The Lord is moving forward with His plans to return.

I am reminded of the words that Jesus spoke in Matthew 24:29-31, 33-44 (emphasis added):

*Immediately after the tribulation of those days the sun will be darkened, and the moon will not give its light; the stars will fall from heaven, and the powers of **the heavens will be shaken**. Then the sign of the Son of Man will appear in heaven, and then all the tribes of the earth will mourn, and they will see the **Son of Man coming on the clouds of heaven with power and great glory**. And He will send His angels with a great sound of a trumpet, and they will gather together His elect from the four winds, from one end of heaven to the other....*

*So you also, **when you see all these things, know that it is near—at the doors!** Assuredly, I say to you, this generation will by no means pass away till all these things take place. Heaven and earth will pass away, but My words will by no means pass away. But of that day and hour no one knows, not even the angels of heaven, but My Father only. But as the days of Noah were, so also will the* *coming of the Son of Man be. For as in the days before the flood, they were eating and drinking, marrying and giving in marriage, until the day that Noah entered the ark, and did not know until the flood came and took them all away, so also will the coming of the Son of Man be. Then two men will be in the field: one will be taken and the other left. Two women will be grinding at the mill: one will be taken and the other left. Watch therefore, for you do not know what hour your Lord is coming. But know this, that if the master of the house had known what hour the thief would come, he would have watched and not allowed his house to be broken into. **Therefore you also be ready, for the Son of Man is coming at an hour you do not expect.***

Better get ready!

There is a whole lot of shaking going on!

Prayers

Prayer of Salvation

Perhaps you would like to be born again and receive Jesus as your Lord and Savior now. Just pray this prayer out loud:

Father God, I believe that Jesus Christ is the Savior or Messiah. I believe that Jesus is the only begotten Son of God and that He died upon the cross to make payment for my sins. I believe that Jesus was buried in an unused grave, but that after three days He rose again to conquer death and sin. Lord, because I was born a human being I was born a sinner. Lord, I ask You to forgive my sins now in the name of Jesus Christ of Nazareth. God cover my sins with the blood of Jesus; forgive me now. Amen.

Prayer of Impartation and Activation and of 20/20 Spiritual Vision

At this moment I bless my God and the Father of my Lord Jesus Christ, who has blessed me with every spiritual blessing in the heavenly places in Christ. And I pray that the God of my Lord Jesus Christ, the Father of glory, may give unto me the spirit of wisdom and revelation in the knowledge of Him. Lord, I ask in the name of Jesus Christ of Nazareth that the eyes of my spirit might receive supernatural understanding and become enlightened.

I ask, Father, that I may know what is the hope of Your calling upon my life and comprehend what are the riches of the glory of the Lord's inheritance in me. Lord, reveal to me what is the exceeding greatness of Your power toward me, because I believe. Lord, release to me the revelatory understanding according to the working of Your mighty power which You worked in Christ Jesus as He rose from the dead and You seated Him at Your right hand in the heavenly places.

Father, You placed the Lord Jesus far above every principality and power and might and dominion and every name that is named, not only in this age but also in that which is to come. Lord, make known to me all of the fullness and unsearchable riches of Christ. Help me to see and comprehend what is the fellowship of the mystery, which from the beginning of the ages has been hidden in God who created all things through Jesus Christ

For this reason I bow my knees to the Father of our Lord Jesus Christ, from whom the whole family in heaven and earth is named. And I ask You, Lord, that You would grant unto me according to the riches of His glory, that I may be strengthened with might through Your Spirit in my soul and inner man. Lord, I pray that Christ may dwell in my heart through faith; that I will become rooted and grounded in the love of God.

Lord, I ask that I might comprehend with all the saints what is the width and length and depth and height—and to personally know and experience the love of Christ, which passes all knowledge, that I may be filled with all the fullness of God. And I thank You, Lord, who is able to do exceedingly abundantly above all that I can ask or think, according to the power of Your Spirit that works within me.

Lord, I thank You now that You are releasing to me the spirit of wisdom and revelation of Your Kingdom and the mighty effectual working of your power in my life, spirit, soul, and body. Thank You, Lord, that You are opening the eyes of my heart and helping me to see and discern the fullness of your Kingdom as it manifests in my life. And to You, Lord, be all the glory in the church by Christ Jesus to all generations, forever and ever. Amen.

Prayer to Make the Secret Place Your Dwelling Place

Lord, Your word teaches me that when I choose to live in the secret place of the Most High that I shall abide under the shadow of the Almighty. Father, today I decree and say of the Lord: You are my refuge and my fortress, You are my God; and I choose at this moment to trust in You!

I thank You, Father, that You shall surely deliver me. You will protect me and keep me under Your feathers and under Your wings; and in Your mighty hand I choose to take refuge, and strength. Lord, Your word and truth shall be my defense, my shield, and my buckler. In You, Father, I will trust.

I shall fear no evil thing nor shall I be fearful of terror by night or of the arrow that flies in the day. No pestilence, sickness, or infirmity shall come near to me. Only with my eyes shall I see the reward of the wicked. I shall live in an abundance of supernatural provision to fulfill my call and God-ordained destiny in You.

Because I choose this day to make the LORD refuge, even the Most High shall be my dwelling place. Therefore, no evil thing shall touch me, nor shall any sickness come near my home.

And I thank You, Father, that You give Your mighty angels charge over me and those in my sphere of influence. You shall faithfully keep me in all Your ways. You order my steps, and You take pleasure in my prosperity and health. I thank You, Lord, that I shall prosper and be in health even as my soul prospers as I choose to make the secret place my dwelling place. Thank You, Lord, that Your angels will lift me up and guard me with their hands to protect and help me.

Lord, I have made the decision and choice to set my spirit, soul, and heart upon You; and therefore, You have promised to deliver me. You have promised to set me upon high, because I have chosen to learn and to know Your name and nature. I shall hear Your voice clearly and be quick to obey. For You are good and Your mercy endures forever for me, and You will never forsake me. You love me with an everlasting love and You enable and empower me to prosper through the finished work of Calvary.

Lord, I choose to call upon You right now; and You promised to answer me. Thank You, Father, that You will be with me in trouble and that You will deliver me and release glory and honor upon my life. Thank You, Father, that You will satisfy me with long life. And thank You, Lord, that You will reveal to me the fullness of Your salvation freely given to me through the finished work of Jesus Christ of Nazareth. In Jesus' name I pray, Amen.

Endnotes

Chapter 3: Shake, Rattle, and Roll

1. "The 10 Worst Earthquakes of 2010," Environment, *China. org.cn*, November 22, 2010, http://www.china.org.cn/ environment/2010-11/22/content_21382447.htm.

Chapter 17: The Glory of God and the Law of Observation

1. Joshua Mills, *Time & Eternity* (London, ON: New Wine International Press, 2011).

2. "Feds Investigating WV Chemical Spill; Thursday, February 6, 2014 @ 05:02 PM gHale," Industrial Safety and Security Source, *isssource.com*, http://www.isssource.com/feds-investigating-wv-chemical-spill/ (accessed January 4, 2015).

Recommended Reading

Unlocking the Hidden Mysteries of the Seer Anointing. Kevin Basconi – King of Glory Printing & Publications.

Unlocking the Hidden Mysteries of the Seer Anointing II: The Blessings of Psalm 24. Kevin Basconi – King of Glory Printing & Publications.

The Sword of the Lord and the Rest of the Lord. Kevin Basconi – King of Glory Printing & Publications.

31 Word Decrees that Can Revolutionize Your Life. Kevin Basconi – King of Glory Printing & Publications.

The Dancing Hand of God. Dr. James Maloney – Answering the Cry Publications.

The Panoramic Seer. Dr. James Maloney – Answering the Cry Publications.

I Believe in Jesus. Kenneth E. Hagin – Kenneth E. Hagin Ministries.

Love the Way to Victory. Kenneth E. Hagin – Kenneth E. Hagin Ministries.

The Name of Jesus. Kenneth E. Hagin – Kenneth E. Hagin Ministries.

Good Morning Holy Spirit. Benny Hinn – Thomas Nelson Publications.

Glory Invasion. David Herzog – Destiny Image

Simple Supernatural: Keys to Living in the Glory Realm. Joshua Mills
– XP Publishing

Secrets of the Argentine Revival. Edward R. Miller –
Peniel Publications.

Angels on Assignment. Roland Buck – Whitaker House Publications.

Angels: Knowing Their Purpose Releasing Their Power. Charles
Capps – Harrison House.

The Sword of the Lord
& The Rest of the Lord

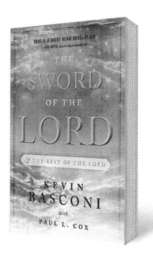

This book *The Sword of the Lord & The Rest of the Lord* was birthed on the Day of Atonement in 2011 and completed on the Day of Atonement in 2012.

Kevin was taken up into the heavenly realms and began to see a tremendous storm full of ominous black clouds moving across the horizon. After some time Kevin witnessed the sky split open and saw the Lord Jesus Christ decent towards the earth upon a mighty white stallion. Jesus was accompanied by millions upon millions of angelic beings who were arrayed for battle. The Lord of Hosts and these millions of angels began to confront the darkness and the billowing storm below. This book is a vivid depiction of those events.

Co-Authored with Paul Cox.

$20.00

SALE $15.00

Unlocking the Hidden Mysteries of the Seer Anointing

This book contains the teachings the revelations that the Lord has given Kevin over the last 12 year about the seer anointing. We are living in a God ordained moment of time when the seer realm is being released by grace to God's friends (whosoever). This book is designed to help God's people unlock the hidden mysteries of the seer anointing in their lives by understanding the idiosyncrasies of the seer anointing in a Christ centered and sound biblical manner. It is a very through biblical teaching that also is replete with dozens of prayers of activation for the reader (seers).

$20.00

SALE $15.00

Unlocking the Hidden Mysteries of the Seer Anointing II
The Blessings of Psalm 24

In the new book, *Unlocking the Hidden Mysteries of the Seer Anointing and the Blessings of Psalm 24*, Kevin Basconi continues to open up the hidden mysteries of the seer anointing. This book is a sequel to Kevin's first book on the seer anointing. In it he shares a set of powerful testimonies of angelic visitations and supernatural experiences that were released from the realms of Heaven. On February 25th, 2014 Kevin had a powerful visitation of the spirit of wisdom and revelation and was launched into a seer experience. The Seer Anointing and the Blessings of Psalm 24 is a MUST READ! This amazing new book is a great read and it is full of Kingdom keys and revelation from Psalm 24 and other places that can help you to activate and accelerate the seer gift and anointing in your life.

~~$20.00~~

SALE $15.00

31 Word Decrees
That Will Revolutionize Your Life
2014 Version

This new 2014 version has been edited and revised! It includes a new bonus word Decree! Forward by Paul Cox.

This little book was birthed or "breathed into existence" by the Holy Spirit. Kevin Basconi has been speaking God's word over his life since he was saved, and delivered from a lifestyle of addiction and sin. In short order the Lord transformed Kevin's life and took him from poverty to prosperity, and from bondage to freedom, from sickness to health.

~~$9.00~~

SALE $8.00

The Seer Anointing &
The Blessings of Psalm 24 CD

In this 2 Cd activation message, *The Seer Anointing & The Blessings of Psalm 24*, Kevin Basconi shares several powerful supernatural encounters concerning the seer anointing. These testimonies have taken place over the last decade as the Lord has released to Kevin understanding and revelation about the seer anointing. On February 25th, 2014 Kevin experienced a powerful angelic visitation in Moravian Falls, North Carolina. In the glory realms that resulted from this supernatural experience Kevin received revelatory understanding from the Spirit of the Lord from Psalm 24. In this message Kevin shares that prophetic word about God's imminent intentions to empower His friends (seers)..

~~$12.00~~

SALE $9.00

Prophetic Worship CD

This worship Cd, *River Of Glory Prophetic Worship,* was recorded live on Saturday, November 2nd, 2014 at Christ Triumphant Church. (All sales benefit widows and orphans). We believe that the glory that was present in this session is attached to this digitally re-mastered recording. Psalmist David Salinas ushered in the glory of God during the worship in this meeting. Then Kevin was actually taken up into the throne room. Kevin began to decree the things that he was seeing in the heavenly realms. We believe that as Kevin decrees the supernatural things that he witnessed in the Throne room on this Mp3, you can also receive your miracle and healing as you listen and soak to the worship and spontaneous decrees of heaven.

~~$19.99~~

SALE $12.00

Activating Your
20/20 Spiritual Vision CD

In this message, *Activating Your 20/20 Spiritual Vision*, Kevin shares several keys that can help you to establish your seer gift and your 20/20 spiritual senses. It is imperative the we become diligent to hear the voice of the Lord and to see what God is doing in our lives at this hour. It is imperative the you develop and build up your ability to discern both good and evil each and every day according to the principle of Hebrews 5:14; Solid food belongs to those who are mature, those who by reason of use have their senses exercised to discern both good and evil. God is seeking to heal and open the spiritual eyes and spiritual ears of His people at this hour. We believe that this message and the prayer of impartation at the end can help spark such a supernatural metamorphosis in your life too! You can learn to discern and activate your 20/20 spiritual senses and vision enabling you to recreate Christ in your sphere of influence. Amen!

$12.00

SALE $10.00

Understanding The Shabbat and Rosh Chodesh CD

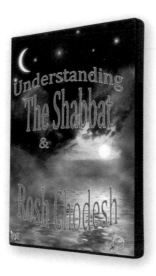

In this double Cd teaching; *A Practical Understanding of The Shabbat and Rosh Chodesh*, Kevin Shares his heart and a basic look at the weekly Sabbath rest and the monthly appointed time of Rosh Chodesh. This scriptural teaching can give you a basic overview of these two important appointed times to come and present yourself before the Lord. There are weekly and monthly times that the Scriptures call us to come before the Lord to receive His blessings and to honor or hallow the Lord. This understanding is a basic key to entering into the rest of the Lord and receiving the supernatural favor of God.

$12.00

SALE $9.00

Entertaining The Heavenly Realms
Worship CD

Entertaining the Heavenly Realms featuring Psalmist David Salinas & Friends. This digitally Re-Mastered Cd features over 79 minutes of heavenly soaking and worship music digitally captured at the new International Ministry Apostolic Equipping Center's Worship Room, right from the heart of Moravian Falls, North Carolina.

~~$15.00~~

SALE $12.00

The Magnificent Holy Spirit
3 CD Mini School

This is a Mini School on the Holy Spirit! These simple Biblical teachings can help you to grow into mature sons and daughters of the Most High God according to the principle of Romans 8: 14: "For as many as are led by the Spirit of God, these are sons of God."

~~$19.99~~

SALE $12.99

This book was prepared for printing by

King of Glory Printing & Publishing

Our goal is to help unpublished authors facilitate printing of their manuscripts in a professional and economical way. If you have a manuscript you would like to have printed, contact us:

336-818-1210
or
828-320-3502

PO BOX 903
Moravian Falls, NC 28654

www.kingofgloryministries.org